Whitefaced Woodland Sheep Society
Flock Profiles

Philip Onions

CORONA BOOKS

First published in the United Kingdom in 2017
by Corona Books UK
www.coronabooks.com

ISBN 978-0-9932472-7-9

Cover photograph by James Onions

All other photos by Philip, James or Katie Onions except
p.18 (first picture) by Martha Ford
p.65 (first and second pictures), p.68 and p.70 courtesy of Jill Thorp
p.72 (first picture) from *Live Stock of the Farm Volume IV: Sheep*, Bryner Jones, C. (Gresham: London, 1916)
p.72 (second picture) and p.73 from *Westmorland Agriculture*, Garnett, Frank W. (Titus Wilson: Kendal 1912)

Book and cover design by Lewis Williams
www.lewiswilliams.com

These profiles are expanded versions of ones previously published in the
Whitefaced Woodland Sheep Society newsletters.

CONTENTS

INTRODUCTION

The Whitefaced Woodland is one of the larger and more distinctive hill breeds of sheep. Both ewes and rams are horned. The rams carry a heavy spiral of horn, while the ewes tend to have a single curve in theirs. They are white faced with a pink nose and white legs, although a small amount of speckling may be seen on their noses and they may have dark or black stripes on their hooves. Their wool is finer than that of many hill breeds. The Whitefaced Woodland is known for its long, meaty tail. The tails of the tups should be left undocked, whereas those of the ewes are docked.

The breed originated in the Woodlands of Hope, an area that once reached much further beyond the small Derbyshire town of Hope than it does today. The Whitefaced Woodland is an amalgamation of several breeds that themselves no longer exist, predominantly the Woodland and the Pensitone (named after the town), but also the Craven and Whitefaced Glossop and the Limestone of Derbyshire. It is closely related to the Lonk, Swaledale and Cheviot breeds.

Today the Whitefaced Woodland is classed as a rare breed by the Rare Breeds Survival Trust (RBST), and the Whitefaced Woodland Sheep Society has long been established with the aim of preserving and promoting the breed. Its membership is open to those who keep or breed the sheep, and to anyone else with an interest in these superb sheep.

Some years ago now, when Rob Ford, the then chair of the Whitefaced Woodland Sheep Society, came up with the idea of a series of flock profiles to promote members' flocks, I jumped at the chance to volunteer to do them. For me, as a relative newcomer to the breed, it gave me the chance to meet some of the people behind the names, and to ask the questions that I had always wanted to ask. Rob was concerned that there were many Woodland breeders spread around the country, who worked on in isolation, almost, to protect this ancient rare breed, but who rarely had the opportunity to 'compare notes' with other breeders. We hoped the flock profiles would serve to promote the breed, to promote the flocks and breeders concerned, and to enable information and knowledge to be shared for the benefit of the whole group and for the improvement of the breed.

The resulting flock profiles are collected here together for the first time, along with some related introductory or explanatory pieces of writing. The fourteen profiles are presented in chronological order (and not in any way order of importance), from the first, which is my own flock profile, to the most recent.

Each profile has been an interesting learning process for me, and I have met some wonderful people in the society. I would like to take this opportunity to thank everyone who has given up their free time to share their experiences with the rest of the group.

Of course, nothing stays constant and all the flocks have changed to some extent since their profiles were compiled. For this reason, the dates of all the profiles are included and should be borne in mind when reading them. Sadly, some flocks and some people mentioned here are no longer with us. This book is dedicated to all Woodland breeders, past and present.

1. THE KEER FALLS FLOCK

I decided to start with my own flock profile. I have done this for one reason, and one reason only, and that is that I was brought up to believe that you should never expect other people to do something for you, that you were not prepared to do yourself. So, I wanted members of the group who I was asking to volunteer to be profiled to see that I was prepared to put my own modest efforts forward too. Now you can all see that I was no expert myself when I began! Because of what I have learned along the way, my own flock has developed since this was written.

PROFILE - THE KEER FALLS FLOCK

Flock prefix: Keer Falls

Year pedigree flock formed: 2001

Size of pedigree flock: Medium (21-50)

Name of breeder: Philip Onions

Address:
Keer Falls Forest Farm
Arkholme
Carnforth
Lancs LA6 1AP

Telephone: 01524 221019 / 07806 700179

email: philip@keerfalls.co.uk

website: www.keerfalls.co.uk

Date of profile: 8th June 2009

Killybawn Nolo, 4 Shear

Breeding Policy

Firstly we wanted to secure only tups with the ARR/ARR genotype. Then we are breeding for size, strength and power. I want a big strong animal with good teeth, legs and muscle. I am looking for the animal to be tall at the shoulder, but with a meaty back end too. These are hill sheep, so I want them to be hardy, but this is only proved by time, so I like ewes that have survived my ruthless cull policy! As for looks, I don't want horns that curl too tightly to the head (a fault of some of Nolo's lambs), nor do I want horns that flyaway like goat horns. I don't want sheep, especially tups, with black spots if possible.

Marketing Policy

I am looking to improve the quality of the flock, so only the tup lambs from the very best ewes are kept entire. All the others are reared as wethers and sold as organic, farm assured, rare breed lamb direct from the farm in freezer packs. Poor gimmers may go the same way; the best are kept for breeding. Cast ewes may be used on commercial tups such as the Texel, if strong enough, or are sent to auction for killing. I rarely sell breeding stock at auction, as I am not

happy with their quality meeting my high standards yet, but I may sell stock privately, so contact me if you are interested in seeing them for yourself.

Showing Achievements

No showing achievements, because I am not yet confident enough with the quality of my stock to show them yet.

A gimmer hogg

Farm Details

Year started to farm here: 1986
Size of farm:
Group C (51 - 100 ha)
Land classification: LFA
Farm type: Beef and sheep
Other crops: Some poultry
Other breeds of livestock kept:
Sheep: Texel crosses,
Mules, Swaledales, Jacob
crosses, Wendsleydales and
Woodland crosses.
Cattle: Aberdeen Angus
crosses.

Description of Farm

Keer Falls Forest Farm is an organic beef and sheep hill farm that straddles the county boundaries of Lancashire and South Lakeland, Cumbria. The farm has a rich biodiversity that includes heavily-rushed pastures, steep hills, flowering meadows, woods and copses, riverside, streams, river, lakes and ponds. At the moment, all the fields are down as permanent pasture. The grassland has been unimproved for many years and is acidic, low in fertility and species rich. No inorganic fertilisers are used at all. No chemical sprays are used at all. All feeds used are GMO free (the farm is GMO free) and 100% organic.

Flock Management – General Details

The flock is managed organically to Soil Association Standards. These Standards are complex and comprehensive, but are aimed at achieving a high level of general health and immunity to keep the whole flock healthy. Rotation and other management practices are aimed at reducing the need to worm sheep. The organic farmer must treat a sick animal using veterinary advice. However, routine use of wormers is prohibited. Flukers are permitted on this farm under derogation from the Soil Association, because the land is so wet and fluke is a recognised problem. Heptavac-P is also permitted as part of the overall health plan. All livestock on the farm were also Bluetongue vaccinated in 2008. Copper is the only permitted mineral on the farm, because blood tests showed a deficiency. Copper boluses are administered in the second half of ewe pregnancy as per instructions. No other routine treatments are used, except a footbath to control footrot.

Four of the fields at Keer Falls

2. THE KILLYBAWN FLOCK

WOODLANDS IN NORTHERN IRELAND

Despite the wild, windy squalls that were hurling themselves against the high sides of our ancient van as we sat on the dockside at Cairnryan awaiting the ferry across the Irish Sea, it was with a real sense of excitement that we anticipated seeing Alan Dickson's Killybawn flock of Whitefaced Woodlands. This is potentially one of the most important flocks in the UK. Why? Because, if for no other reason, Alan stands as the lone guardian over a flock which provides a priceless insurance to us all if the mainland were to be ravished once more by a disease like Foot and Mouth. Take it from me, as someone who farmed on the edge of Cumbria and saw the result of the disease on a neighbouring farm, if ever it did to the High Peak what it did to Cumbria, then we will all need these isolated, satellite flocks if we are to stand any chance to conserve this important breed.

Your 'roving reporter' is pleased to report that he was far from disappointed by his trip. Alan and his family are doing a superb job of maintaining three important bloodlines of high quality pedigree sheep, more details of which follow in the flock profile below.

Although my son James and I only had time to spend the weekend in Northern Ireland, Alan, his father Bill and all of their family made us very welcome. In fact, it is true to say that everyone we met in this fabulous part of the UK made us feel extremely welcome.

For those of you who have never visited Northern Ireland, or who have not been there for many years, Belfast is a really modern city now, with outstandingly good roads and cutting edge architecture. For those interested in shopping, James and I wandered awestruck through a very sophisticated shopping centre filled with the most chic designer boutiques, where our rustic charms stuck out like sore thumbs, and I'm sure that we ended up with half of the security guards following us. But then, I didn't want a Rolex, and Tommy Hilfiger designer underpants wouldn't match our wellies and woolly hats anyway!

The countryside of the north east side of the country is much more to our taste, however. I had the very real sense that everyone there was in touch with their rural heritage. Bill later explained the very enlightened planning rules, which actively encourage scattered development, which allows families to stay together near to their family farms and heritage. Bill had been turned down on a planning application to build an extra family cottage next to his own, at the end of the drive to Alan's, because there were already too many houses in the area! Around here you might, and I stress might, get planning permission there as 'infill'.

There were a huge number of original and unique new buildings going up everywhere, in all kinds of styles. Many of the farms were smaller than you would see around us, with small fields and high natural hedges and clusters of farm buildings attached to most. The relaxed attitude to planning extended to gardens that ranged from grand, stately, formal gardens to the ones that I particularly related to, where the weeds were suppressed by paving over the entire garden with round bales! How very practical!

Alan's farm is immaculately set amongst the rolling drumlins of the area. He inherited it from his grandmother, and it was apparently run down and almost derelict when he took it on; but you wouldn't know that now, because Alan and his wife have turned it into a modern spacious family home to be proud of!

Alan works as an accountant in Belfast, and Bill is a retired teacher, although I suspect he is possibly busier now with various projects around the farm than he was before! He's built a large barn and several outbuildings, and has ambitious plans to reseed all the fields, which are small and steep. Bill keeps a flock of pedigree Rouge De L'Ouest sheep, and they have found that the Rouge tup put onto a cast WW ewe or a shearling that they don't want to breed from produces an outstanding butchers' lamb, and Alan now has a keen following of commercial farmers looking to procure his older WW ewes to put to terminal sires. And I can see why!

Alan is not alone in admiring the Woodland, though, in these parts. He tells me that he has sold ewes to a number of local breeders who, sadly, have not chosen to join our society or to maintain the pedigrees, but who nonetheless, breed the sheep true. Is this a new Hill Register in the making in Northern Ireland, I wonder? I actually passed a field with a flock containing a few Woodlands on the dash back to the ferry with our newly acquired tup. I have to say that if you ignore the mountain of paperwork, importing a tup from Alan back into England, was easy! So come on everyone, let's all help Alan in his modest, but noble attempt to conserve the breed in Northern Ireland!

PROFILE - THE KILLYBAWN FLOCK

Flock prefix: Killybawn

Year pedigree flock formed: 1991

Size of pedigree flock: Medium (21-50)

Name of breeder: Alan Dickson

Address:
35 Killybawn Road
Saintfield
Co. Down
Northern Ireland
BT247JP

Telephone:
02844 830469 / 07710 348129

email: alanw.dickson@tiscali.co.uk

Date of profile: 3rd October 2009

Alan Dickson and his father Bill with a shearling

Breeding Policy

Alan maintains three specific bloodlines in his flock, the Beckermond Ross, White House Acclaim and Riffham bloodlines. Each year Alan and Bill select the best tup lambs from each line to keep pure, and then castrate the others. Alan selects breeding stock by size and conformation, then he is looking for horns that are growing flat from the top of the head (not away as a goat's might). He does not want horns that point too far forward or that are growing too close to the head. Although Alan wants big sheep, it is important to him that they are not long in the leg. Finally, Alan wants all his sheep to have fine, long wool with a good crimp in it.

The three tups selected from the three bloodlines: from left to right,
Riffhams, Beckermond Ross and Whitehouse Acclaim

One of Alan's gimmers, showing the fine, long wool with a good crimp,
which is popular with spinners

Marketing Policy

Presently Alan is struggling to market his tups in Northern Ireland, and Bluetongue restrictions make it very difficult to return sheep from England to Northern Ireland if they fail to reach a fair price at auction. This makes maintaining the flock unnecessarily difficult! However, he regularly sells some tups and all of his spare ewes in the province itself.

A Killybawn gimmer and two of the tups
Note the closeness of the horns to the head and the long open fleece

The head of one of the tups
Note the 'Roman nose' and that the horns come away cleanly from his face

Killybawn ewes

Showing Achievements

Alan has numerous showing achievements up against rare and commercial breeds. Of special note are his awards for First Place Female Hogget and Second for his Ram Lamb at the Balmoral or Royal Ulster Agricultural Show (the biggest one in Northern Ireland) and at Ballymena Second Place for 'Ewe of any age'.

Farm Details

Year started to farm here: 1840
Size of farm: Group B (21 - 50 ha)
Land classification: None LFA
Farm type: Sheep. *Other crops*: None
Other breeds of livestock kept: Rouge De L'Ouest Sheep

Description of Farm

35 Killybawn Road is a small, family farm that has been in the family since 1840, or thereabouts. Once it was a show farm for their dairy of 14 cows that were then milked by hand – this was in Alan's grandmother's day. Now the farm is run more as a hobby, for Bill's pedigree Rouge De L'Ouest flock and Alan's pedigree Whitefaced Woodlands. Both gentlemen enjoy showing their sheep, but don't take the job too seriously. I get the impression that Bill's Rouges take priority over Alan's Woodlands if they can't show both at the same show for some reason. The farm is made up of small, fertile fields of steep, rolling drumlins. They have high hedges and freely draining soil.

Flock Management

At present, the flock does not receive extra feed during the winter, because the mild climate maintains grass growth for longer than some on higher ground can expect. Since the addition of Bill's big new shed, they can lamb inside. Their biggest problem at present seems to be that the ewes are a little too fat at tupping and this has pulled down lambing percentages, but they are working on the problem. All sheep coming from Northern Ireland enjoy MVA accreditation because the country is free of the disease. They are also outside the Bluetongue area. Their sheep are all vaccinated, and they are happy to fluke and worm sheep at the buyer's request before dispatch. Gimmer lambs are not put to the tup in their first year. Three tup lambs, one from each bloodline, are kept entire each year, but not worked until they reach a good size. Alan is considering AI in the future, given the geographic isolation point and is keen to find out if other breeders are currently using it, and with what success?

Killybawn tups enjoying the sun

3. JAMES GILL'S FLOCK

THE MAN OF THE MOMENT

Up here on the limestone hills around Hutton Roof, we don't hold much with this celebrity culture that seems to obsess our society. Oh, I've heard that 'Robbie Williams' on the tractor radio and the lad seems to be able to hold a tune, and I'm told that that 'David Beckham' can kick a football, but what the heck Paris Hilton is all about, escapes me!

On the other hand, if there is someone worthy of some attention, then for me it has to be James Gill! James has smashed the record yet again with his ram selling for the highest price at the annual Bretton Mill Whitefaced Woodland sale.

Having admired the size of his sheep for many years now, the question that I most wanted to ask was 'What on Earth do you feed them on?' But having visited James and spent a couple of hours with him, I realise just how naïve this question is, because if there is a magic ingredient that can explain away all of James' success, then it is quite obviously James himself. James is a professional shepherd, in every sense of the word. It is his no nonsense professionalism and attention to detail which is the key to his success

As soon as my son and I entered James' field, James focused on his sheep; a soft whistle and his dog was away, gathering them up. Modestly James mentions that he was once on *One Man and His Dog*. Then he goes on to tell us about the breeding behind each sheep. He knows them all well, but doesn't fuss about naming them. James points out sheep after sheep, discussing the best and worst features of each animal critically but honestly.

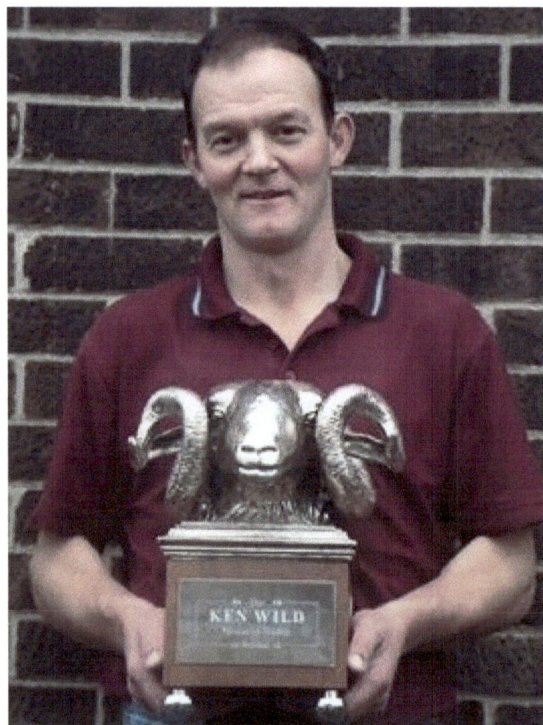

James Gill with the Ken Wild Memorial Trophy, which he won in the 2009 Whitefaced Woodland Sale at Bretton Mill

I struggle to get a clear photo of his tup lamb, so James politely waits a moment, then gathers them with his dog and snatches the tup from the flock as they pass. Holding it, he calmly tells me all about its breeding and its qualities – it is out of that Paul Thorp tup that he just sold at Bretton Mill.

Then he opens its mouth, and like an electric shock I realise just how young the lamb is and it's huge! He then tells me that it is only seven months old!

A master class in keeping and breeding Whitefaced Woodlands then followed, and all I could think of at the end was that if all Woodlands were like this, every sheep farmer would want to keep them and it would not be a rare breed!

This tup must be the way forward for the whole breed!

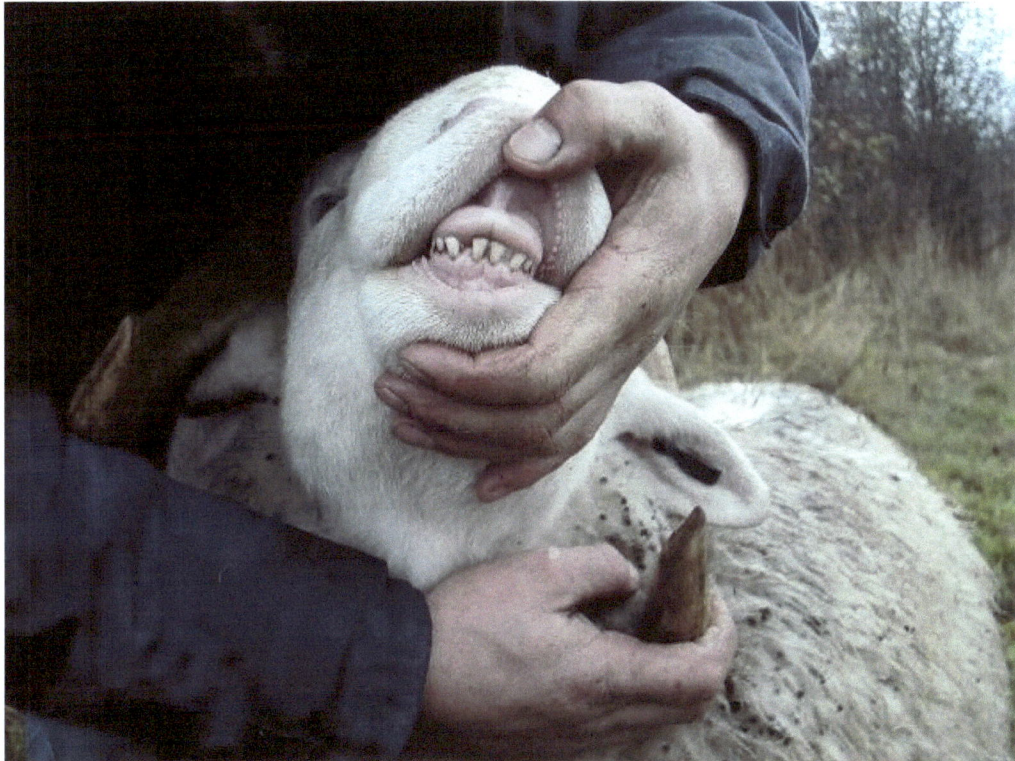

James' seven-month-old tup lamb out of Paul Thorp's tup
This is a seven-month old lamb!

PROFILE - JAMES GILL'S FLOCK

Flock details: Hill registered

Size of pedigree flock: Medium (21-50)

Name of breeder: James Gill

Address:
6 Green Acres
Hoyland
Barnsley
South Yorkshire
S74 0HL

Telephone: 01226 743663/07984 682272

Date of profile: 24th October 2009

James Gill with a shearling ewe

Breeding Policy

James has a clear idea of what he is looking for - above all else, he wants size. The sheep have to have the frame or bone to carry that weight. When James first bought Paul Thorp's tup, what he liked most about it was that it had a 'right, good back'. 'The back has got to be straight – no dip at the shoulder – and a tight skin,' he says. That means a tightly packed closed fleece that sheds water and keeps the sheep warm. 'And good on his feet; that takes bone, good bone.' When it comes to the head, James likes the Roman nose, he shyly admits. He likes it to be broad too.

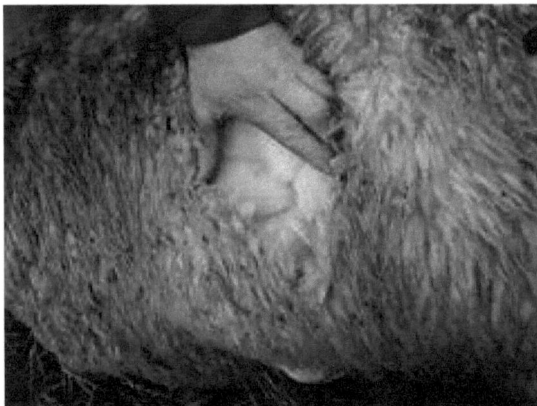

The tup lamb that James showed me has many of the qualities that he is looking for. It has the size, a straight back and a broad Roman nose. It has a tight skin, strong bone and good feet. It has kinder horns than its father too, and James thinks that it looks like these horns will not be too close to its head as they grow.

'If he had a fault,' James says of the tup that he's just sold, 'then I would have to say that his horns were too hard. The one that I bought from Edward Lees has kinder horns. I'm hoping that he'll make his lambs' horns a bit kinder too; it's always the tup that does that, isn't it?' He explains that for the horns to be kinder, they have to be narrower.

Part of the breeding policy is a very strong cull programme. With limited land available to him, James can't afford to keep any sheep that does not have a place in his breeding programme. Store lambs go in July, cast ewes follow quickly; any ewes with qualities that don't measure up to the rest have to go too. All rams have to go after two years, or else they might end up back on their daughters. 'I didn't want to let that tup go, but I had to make room for his son.'

James tries to keep five or six of his best gimmers to breed from each year. He has kept ten ewes off Paul Thorp's tup and six gimmers; that's all he has room for.

James' new seven-month-old tup lamb out of the Champion Paul Thorp tup
Note the head shape from the side and front

The ewes running with the tup lamb

James' Champion tup bred by Paul Thorp. Note the strong, thick horns.

James' new tup from Edward Lees

The same attention to detail goes into the selection of gimmers for breeding too. Once again, James is working on a good-sized frame carrying a sheep with a good mouth, tight skin, good head and horns. The gimmer pictured below is one that James particularly rates highly. Of particular note is size and straightness of back. It is also interesting to see that although it has a Roman nose, this is not as pronounced as in some others, but overall, James feels that this is one of the best.

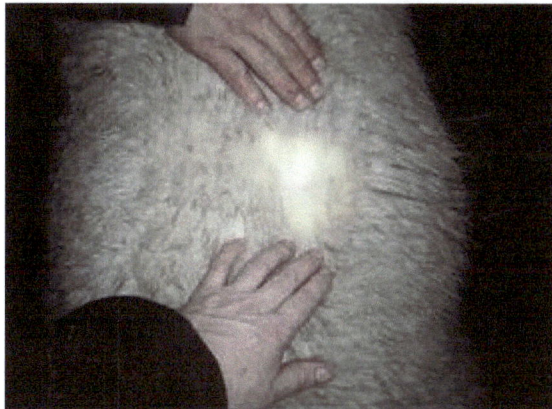

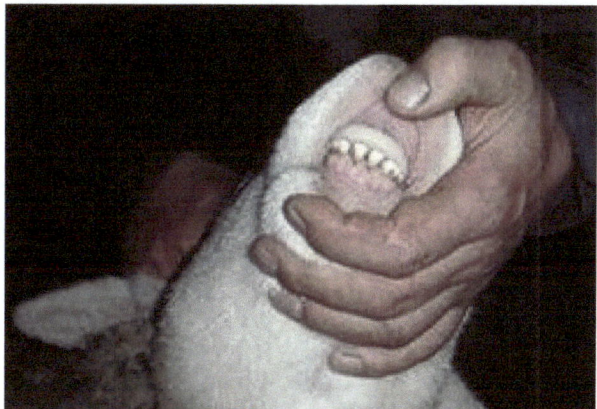

A gimmer lamb of seven months
Bottom left: the ginmmer has a good tight skin
Bottom right: the gimmer's baby teeth

The gimmer lamb pictured here on the right, though, James feels has a better face, but it is let down by a poorer more open fleece.

Marketing Policy

James has a 'no nonsense' marketing policy too. His full-time work as a shepherd doesn't give him enough time to trail about, so all lambs not wanted for breeding go as store lambs in July to the farmer he works for, who puts them through the farm shop. Tups are sold after two years' work, to prevent in-breeding, or as shearlings for the same reason.

Showing Achievements

These are too numerous to mention them all. Most notable are: Supreme Champion of Woodlands twice at the Hope Show; Champion of Champions twice at Hope with Paul Thorp's tup; Champion Woodland tup twice at Hayfield; and Champion four times at Bretton Mill!

James' dog gathers some sheep through the autumnal mists
Note the size of the ewes!

Farm Details

Year started to farm here: 2006
Size of farm: Group A (1 - 20 ha)
Land classification: LFA
Farm type: Sheep
Other crops/breeds of livestock kept: None

Description of Farm

James used to work as a shepherd in the High Peak. He originally got sheep of his own, so that he could train his dogs without upsetting his employers if the dog got over enthusiastic. He kept Woodlands to avoid them getting mixed up when run with his employer's black-faced sheep. When James moved to Hoyland, he got a field of his own. It is quite large, flat, free-draining, fertile land that grows grass well. In winter James is able to graze several other fields, including the large twelve plus acre silage field above. He intends to take these sheep off and to put just six gimmers on it to winter! James has built a very useful small lambing shed in his field, where he can keep his lambing sheep that have problems. Next to his lambing shed he has a shipping container for about fifty bales of hay, which will need refilling before spring, and nearby a round gathering pen to hold sheep while he trains his dog – he keeps a few well-dogged half-bred sheep in this field over winter to train dogs on. As soon as they saw his dog they ran to us, as well-dogged sheep do. Some of these were Woody crosses.

Flock Management

James' sheep are managed carefully to encourage them to fully reach the potential of their breeding. Lambs are reared only from the best parents. Lambs are grown on without check or hindrance. Grass is managed to keep it fresh, with sheep being moved onto fresh ground every six weeks or so during summer – the field is divided up to allow this. All sheep have access to powdered minerals at all times. All get multivit drenches twice a year. Lambs are wormed every month starting in May, when they also get a multivit drench. Ewes are wormed twice a year. There is no fluke problem on the farm. All sheep are in the Heptavac system.

Because James sells his store lambs and unwanted sheep in July, this will free up the land for the ewes to get back into top condition. James does not believe that sheep can be too fit at tupping. James' sheep were all in superb condition this October; I could not feel any of their backbones at all. James achieves a 175% lambing rate. All ewes are tailed before tupping and kept 'clean' through to lambing.

James with the tup purchased from Edward Lees at the Bretton Mill Sale

At tupping time, 18th October onwards, the ewes are moved off James' land to his over-wintering land to rest it and allow the grass to grow back for lambing. James would like to spread slurry on his land then, as he used to, but the new NVZ rules prevent this now, and he doesn't want to spread slurry in the spring where his sheep are to graze. No other fertilisers are used. The ewes are moved around several small fields as they eat up the grass. When the pictures here were taken, they were in fields that had held no livestock all summer on a neighbour's land. This neighbour had intended to make hay on some of it, but here it was too rough to mow. The grass was uncut from summer.

James does not feed corn or cake to any of his sheep, but those brought into the lambing shed may get some sugar beet nuts. With dogs as well trained as James has, he does not need to feed cake to tups to get raddle on them, nor does he use harnesses. James feeds them some very high quality hay in the worst of winter. There was no sign that any of the sheep wanted or needed extra feeding when we were there.

*Ewes are all tailed at tupping time and then kept clean until lambing,
grazing on clean land for the winter*

Shearling ewe out of the champion Paul Thorp tup

*Two older ewes, of special note is that their noses are flatter and their horns not as tight to their heads as with the shearling
pictured above, whose horns are more like her father's in that they hug tightly against the back of the head*

4. THE BECKERMOND FLOCK

Wharfedale and the hillside opposite, home to the Beckermond flock

It was a bleak, wet winter's dawn as I made my way through the snow speckled limestone peaks and dales of Malham Moor to profile the Beckermond flock in Wharfedale. I don't have to delve too deeply into my own sheep's pedigrees before I meet the Beckermond flock prefix, so for me this was a pilgrimage into the history of my own sheep. But for other breeders too, the Beckermond flock and Dr. and Mrs. Harrison have played a huge role in the conservation of the Whitefaced Woodland breed over the past quarter of a century, so this has been a hugely influential flock.

Wharfedale is a 'U' shaped valley, with steep sides climbing above Kettlewell very steeply until they round off over the limestone hills beyond.

This is Swaledale country and that breed still dominates the hills and dales, although here and there Texel tups are working amongst the black-faced flocks, and on the opposite side of the road to the Beckermond flock there was a field of Wensleydale sheep. But despite this, because of various schemes and conservation initiatives, the hills also now contain a scattering of rare breeds such as Long Horn cattle and Belted Galloways as rarer breeds become part of the mainstream; so what could be more appropriate than Whitefaced Woodland sheep on these hills?

PROFILE - THE BECKERMOND FLOCK

Flock prefix: Beckermond

Year pedigree flock formed:
1983 (started farming
here 1985)

Size of pedigree flock:
Medium (21-50)

Name of breeder:
Ric Halsall

Telephone:
01756 760296

email: richalsalls@aol.com

Date of profile:
5th December 2009

Ric Halsall with Beckermond Richard
out of the Riffhams bloodline

Flock History

The Beckermond flock was started by Ross and Avril Harrison in 1983 with two in-lamb ewes. Two more were added a year later from Hardwick Hall. The Harrisons moved up to Wharfedale in 1985, bringing six ewes with them from Staffordshire. Six more ewes were then purchased locally, and the flock then became a closed flock but for the occasional addition of more tups over the years.

The Harrisons, keen on conservation, have set about concentrating on some of the older bloodlines from within the breed. 'We concentrated on avoiding the Cherry Tree and Pickenaze bloodlines in particular, because we felt that they were over represented in the CFB [Combined Flock Book],' Avril told me. 'It's important for the whole breed that we don't get too hung up on just a few of the major bloodlines, otherwise we will end up getting a genetic bottleneck within the breed and this will lead to in-breeding.'

The Beckermond flock is managed in such a way as to maintain rare bloodlines such as Riffhams; with Hawksworth and Belfield through the male line, and Ken Wild's through the female Riffhams line. They also have School Green, Ecolan, Whitehouse Acclaim (which is the Fairbanks line apparently) and Hayridge down through male lines. When talking to Avril, it is clear that she puts the greatest importance over bloodlines, and in the past new additions to the flock have been chosen with bloodlines very much in mind.

Avril was most upset when she found out that Beckermond Whisky Mac from the Ash and Pennine lines was lost to the CFB, because they'd sold his offspring into an unregistered flock.

Ross Harrison was instrumental, with others, in setting up the Whitefaced Woodland Breeders Group in 1986, and the group worked closely with the RBST over the years to help conserve the breed. The Harrisons have contributed at every level within the conservation movement, from showing sheep to sending wool to the wool board for testing and then using that wool to demonstrate the high quality of Woodland fleeces. Ross has judged sheep classes at many shows including the Royal Lancashire and Great Yorkshire shows, as well as shows from Northern Ireland to the smaller local shows. They have many showing successes themselves (see below) and have sold sheep throughout the UK. Avril showed me a list of people and flocks they've sent sheep to over the years and it is very impressive. Avril says that, 'the reward has been to see new flocks started and continue to thrive'.

Ross and Avril Harrison, now in their second retirement, have passed their flock over to Ric Halsall, as the steepness of the land and the size and power of their sheep have become too much for them to cope with any more, and I really don't blame them as I was quite breathless climbing even a small part of the hill myself! Ric, their 'lad' – as they say in these parts – has been helping the Harrisons out ever since he took early retirement in 2002. Unusually, the RBST have agreed to allow Ric to keep the Beckermond prefix because he has bought the entire flock and farms them on the same land in much the same way; usually this can only be done when a flock passes on down through a family.

Left: Whitehouse Acclaim Nathan, the last tup to be bought in, four years ago
Right: Ewes from the Beckermond flock

Breeding Policy

Ric is trying to maintain the bloodlines that Ross and Avril originally set up; however he is also trying to improve the quality of the sheep under his own care. With this in mind, Ric is looking for size and conformation within his group. 'What I look for in a sheep is basically what I look for in a woman,' he laughs. 'I want good looks! I think Woodies are good looking sheep! That's what I look for!'

'So what makes a good Woody, then?' I ask.

'One that stays alive!' he quips back, with typical Dales humour.

'So a bad one would presumably be a dead one,' I laugh.

'Exactly!' he chuckles. I soon come to realise that Ric is a very practically minded man!

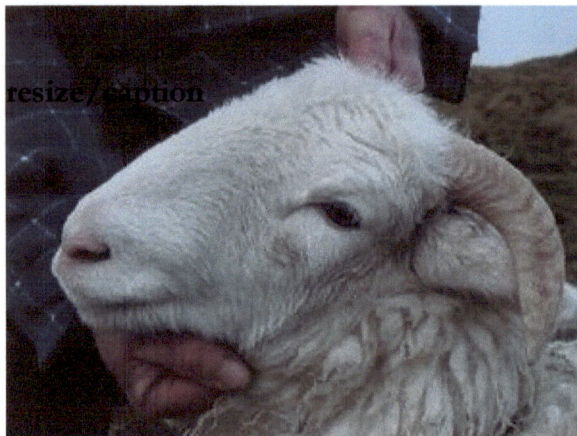

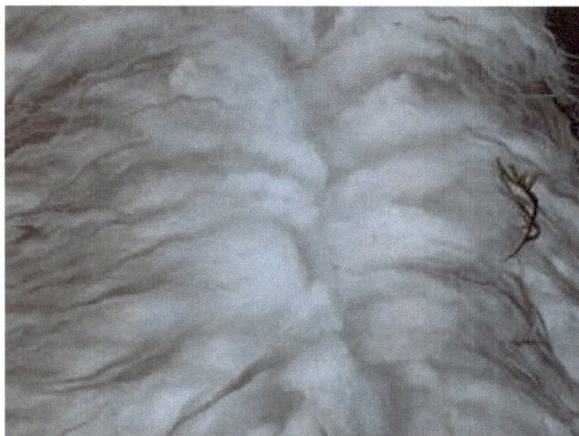

A Beckermond gimmer (photos taken in the rain)
The image on the right shows its long, soft crimp

Marketing Policy

Breeding sheep are sold from the farm or at Skipton's Rare Breed Sale. Tup lambs and unwanted gimmers are sold as stores through Skipton Auction Mart too. Ric told me that last year he castrated most of their male lambs, thinking that they would do better and make more in the store lamb ring, but he also sold some entire. These ram lambs turned out to be bigger than the castrated lambs, even the twins, and made £1/head more! So this year he didn't castrate any!

Showing Achievements

From 1985, they've had huge successes at Great Yorkshire, Midland Counties, Stafford County, York RBST show and sale, and Penistone Sheep fairs with their sheep. Also, from 1987, they've had highly placed fleeces at the Great Yorkshire and Masham Sheep Fairs. The list is very impressive and long, so I asked Avril which showing achievements she was most proud of. She immediately said that it was winning the prize for the Supreme Fleece at the RBST show at Stoneleigh in 1994 and the Champion Fleece at the Great Yorkshire Show in 2007, where she felt that she won on behalf of the Whitefaced Woodland breed against all other breeds.

Avril Harrison and Ric Halsall

The ewe on the right gave the fleece that won Champion Fleece at the Great Yorkshire Show in 2007. Her daughter is on the left.

Farm Details

Year started to farm here: 1985
Size of farm: Group B (21 - 50 ha)
Land classification: LFA, SDA
Farm type: Sheep
Other crops: None
Other breeds of livestock kept: Some Woody crosses

Description of Farm

The farm used by the Beckermond flock rises steeply from 700 to 1750 feet. Most lies within a ring fence, which consists of high, well-maintained dry-stone walls with wall top wire and the remains of an electric ring fence. The two or three lower pastures are flatter with good quality grass, but the upper fields and allotment is steep with coarse, poor quality grazing. The soil is thin, acidic and rocky, but has a wide range of wild flowers and herbs in summer apparently.

Flock Management

Historically, the Beckermond flock has been fed a coarse sheep mix all year around in small quantities; this was to keep the sheep manageable and in the best condition on the poor ground. Ric has kept this practice up, even though there was no shortage of grass when I visited in December it was poor and coarse.

One of the first team of tups out at work, ever mindful of what lurks just below, beyond the fence! (see next picture)

Ric lambs outside at the end of April and into May, but the ewes and their lambs are brought down into two very smart well-made barns for 48 hours before being turned out again. Lambs are sprayed and have temporary ear tags applied and tailed where appropriate; as previously mentioned, tup lambs will now be kept entire. Foxes are not a problem on the farm, and they have no known fluke problem. They are now only Bluetongue vaccinating sheep that they intend to sell. At the time of the visit, the sheep were all in their tupping groups and tups were in harness.

A fresh set of spare tups or 'seconds' is kept to ensure that the 'first' set is up to the job in hand. This second team of tups are all selected from the same bloodlines as the first team, and each is destined to follow the tup whose bloodline he shares. This is a good way to ensure that an entire year's production of each bloodline is guaranteed. The second team tend to be younger tups, allowing them to grow on without being overworked, which is known to stunt young tups that put work ahead of nutrition.

The second team wait, miserably looking on at all the action, ready to be deployed later, eager for their turn!

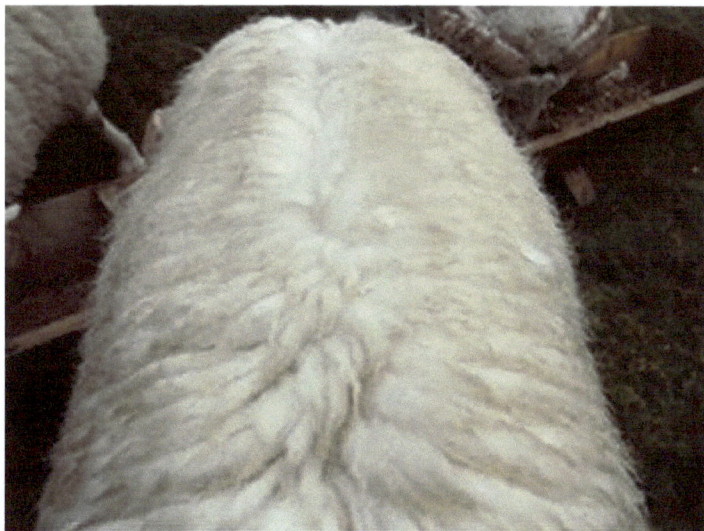

The fleece of one of the second team tups
Note the long, fine open fleece. This high-quality wool
is good for spinners and felt makers.

INTERLUDE: A BRIEF NOTE ON WOOL

It is worth pausing at this point in the flock profiles to note that there are two distinct viewpoints as to what constitutes a 'good' fleece. Whitefaced Woodlands have some of the highest quality wool of any hill breed and a number of breeders are determined to improve or at the very least maintain this reputation. However, for commercial sheep farmers, there is a completely opposing, equally valid, viewpoint. Let me explain.

By law (correct when written in 2009) all sheep farmers are supposed to sell all their wool through the Wool Marketing Board unless they have permission to sell it themselves (which we at Keer Falls do for example). I understand that around here it currently costs somewhere between £1 and £1.50 to get a sheep shorn (I have always done this job myself, so I'm not sure exactly). My neighbour has six hundred sheep, which produced almost three tonnes of wool in 2008, for which they were paid about £150 in total before costs.

*James Gill holds his new tup
while the author prepares to photograph its fleece*

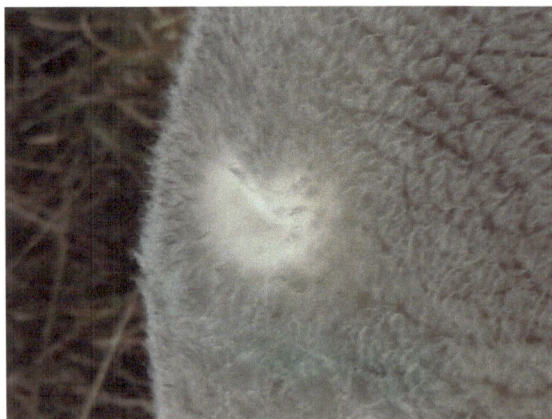

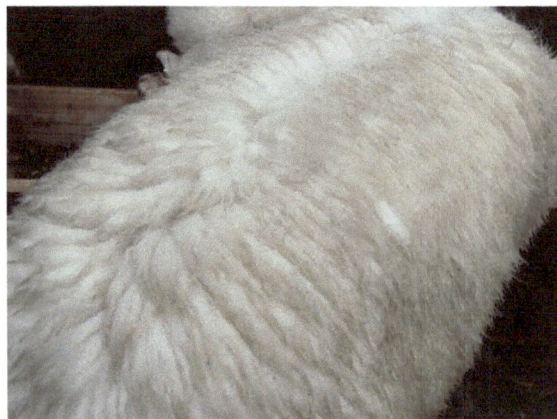

You can see that for the commercial sheep farmer selling wool to the Wool Board, wool is just a problem to be got rid of. As a result, the reality is that commercial sheep breeders want a tight coarse fleece that sheds rainwater quickly; nothing kills more sheep than cold wet weather and mortality is more expensive than even the best quality wool is worth over the lifetime of a long-lived sheep. Their view is better a live sheep, with water-resistant wool, than a dead one, with long, high quality wool. The irony is that this erodes the value of their wool cheque even further, so getting the balance right is the key to success.

*Left: James Gill's tup above, showing a 'good tight fleece'
Right: A Beckermond tup, showing 'good wool' with an open long crimp*

5. THE BELFIELD FLOCK

WOODIES IN THE FOG

As we climbed out of Macclesfield on the Buxton road, a thick curtain of fog engulfed us. It had been foggy since we'd left home, but as the mild humid air reached the remains of the Christmas snows on the hills, it became so dense you could taste it.

I had wanted to visit Neville Belfield's flock over the Christmas holidays so both my children could come with me, but we'd been snowed in from the 20th of December until a week into the new term to anything but 4x4 tractors and quad bikes, and according to 'Sally Traffic' on the radio the road at the 'Cat and Fiddle' had also been shut, so we'd had to leave it.

Neville Belfield bought that tup of James Gill's at the Bretton Mill sale – the record breaking one – and I had been raving to my children James and Katie all about it for some time, and James had seen this tup's seven-month-old ram lamb when we'd profiled James Gill's flock earlier, so he was expecting a giant of a sheep.

'It's big then?' Katie asked with her usual understatement. 'Bigger even than our Woodies?'

'Oh yes!' James replied. 'It's going to be head and shoulders above all the other sheep! Wait and see! We'll see it a mile off!'

'Well he was certainly bigger than the other tups at Bretton Mill when I saw him last!' I agreed.

So we all eagerly jumped into Neville's link box for the tractor ride up the hillside to see this goliath of the Woody world striding down through a flock of presumably awestruck ewes, quaking and cringing at his thunderous passing. But it was not to be…

Now please don't misunderstand me, we were anything but disappointed, it's just that at first this special tup was hard to see, not because there was anything wrong with him – far from it – it was just that all the sheep were so big!

'My God!' Katie exclaimed. 'Look at all of them! They're huge!' (We won't print what James said!)

This is now the fifth flock, including mine, that I have profiled and I have been keeping Woodies for a while now, and seen many sold at sales, but I have never quite experienced the awe that I felt as such a big flock of excellent, giant sheep came quietly and calmly up to us to get a bit of hay on that freezing hillside today! Now these were real sheep, as a neighbour of mine would say.

PROFILE - THE BELFIELD FLOCK

Size of pedigree flock: Large (51-100)
Some hill registered, most not

Name of breeder: Neville Belfield

Address:
69 London Road
Macclesfield

Telephone: 01625 425426

Date of profile: 23rd January 2010

Neville Belfield

Breeding Policy

Since Neville's retirement, he only keeps 80 Woodies, 'just to keep my hand in', so he has been able to concentrate on keeping only the best ewes. He chooses only the biggest sheep, regardless of all else, and then he starts to consider their other features. In the tup, first he starts with the head, 'Everything follows through from the head,' he told me. 'I don't want the horns either too tight to the head, nor flying away. Then I want good, broad shoulders. That's not normal in Woodies, so it is an important point to look for. They need good deep bodies too. They have to stand well; that can be another weakness in Woodies. Then, they have to be good in the mouth, too many of them are overshot. You have to check their mouths.'

'Do you check all their mouths?' I ask. 'Even the ewes?'

'Oh yes, I never buy any sheep without checking its mouth!' he tells me. 'They need good deep jackets too, not too close, but they mustn't part down the middle! You wouldn't like it if someone cut down the back of your jacket on a cold wet day, would you?'

Neville only keeps six male lambs entire each year. He chooses the lambs at birth, which is a really difficult thing to do in my experience. So I asked how he could tell what a tup is going to end up like, when it's born.

Oh it's very hard,' he agreed. 'You can't always get it right. I know who the tup is of course, then I'm very careful which ewes I breed from. They have to be perfect...well as near perfect as I can get – none of them are absolutely perfect – so I select the very best. Then out of the six that I've kept entire, I'll probably only keep a couple. The ones that aren't good enough go to the butchers with all the wethers.'

The fleece above 'parts down the middle', whereas the one below is deep, but 'tight'.

Neville has two tups, the one mentioned above and one that he bred himself. He explained that he sold this tup's father – whom he had bred himself – to a neighbour because he didn't really think him good enough to breed from, but bought back this tup as soon as he saw it. The difference between the two is very small, but there was a huge difference in what Neville paid for them both!

Neville's two tups feed together. The prize-winning tup is on the left, but almost as big is one that's bred from one of his own tups, in the middle of the picture.

33

Neville only keeps tups for two breeding seasons, to stop in-breeding.

Alongside the breeding of pure Whitefaced Woodlands, Neville puts Texel tups on to some of his poorer ewes. Neville is very keen to promote this cross; it does produce an exceptional animal.

'The Woodland and Texel are made for each other,' he preaches to the converted. 'There's nothing quite like it! It's much better than the mule! Don't bother with trying the Bluefaced Leicester on the Woodland though; it's rubbish!' (Note: Since making this comment, Neville has revised his position. Apparently, the cross he dismissed then went on to prove to be the best sheep their new owner had ever had.)

Left: Just one of the many Belfield ewes. Note the strong, straight back and deep body.
Right: Neville's prize winning tup, winner of the Ken Wild Memorial Trophy at the Bretton Mill sale in 2009

Marketing Policy

Neville's daughter farms with his Woody Texel cross ewes, which produce superb fat lambs. She puts shearling Woodies to the Beltex and then older ewes to big Texels. Fat lambs from this cross go through Chelford auction.

Neville sells some ewes every year through the Bretton Mill sale, along with 5-shear ewes and a spare tup or two – look out for the champion tup in a couple of years' time, if you're lucky!

Neville sells all of his WW wethers through a local butcher from Christmas to Easter. The butcher buys solely from Neville and another local Woody breeder during this period. The butcher prefers Woodland wethers at this time of the year, because experience shows that they taste better than other fat lambs available then!

Showing Achievements

Neville told me that he never really had time to show sheep except when he was selling them, but he modestly mentioned that he has won at Bretton Mill a couple of times!

Farm Details
Year started to farm here: 1965
Size of farm: Group C (51 - 100 ha)
Land classification: LFA
Farm type: Sheep
Other crops: None. *Other breeds of livestock kept*: Sheep: Texels

Description of Farm

Neville's farm is a typical modern farm; the farmhouse has been sold and some land is rented off and Neville rents in other land – it's all very complicated, as these things tend to be! The relevant bit to the Woodies is that they are presently kept on a large block of steep hill land about a thousand feet up. It is fertile though, compared with other land that I've seen. The land is free-draining with a number of scattered trees, deep sheltered ravines and high stonewalls topped with neat wall-top wire. 'That's more to keep the walkers and their sledges out than the sheep in!' Neville confides. 'You should have seen it last week. The field was covered with tracks! I wouldn't mind, but they climb over the walls and knock them down!' I totally sympathise as walker after walker marches past us on the road above, chattering loudly and gawping at the farmers feeding the sheep!

Management

All the sheep are drenched for worms and fluke twice a year, once just before tupping. Lambs are wormed twice, once at shearing and once before weaning. All the sheep are in the Heptavac-P system, starting with two injections six weeks apart and then annual boosters. This year all the sheep have had Foot-Vax too; he used to do them every year and it worked very well. The sheep get Crovec and copper in mid-winter. Neville has not dipped for ten years, but he has no experience of Scab here; it should be noted that the field that they were in was within high walls onto highways, with no other sheep in direct contact to Neville's.

The Woodies are kept on a large block of steep land.

The ewes have run with the record-breaking tup from the 10th of December to lamb in May, when there is plenty of daylight to allow lambing outside. The second tup was let go about seventeen days later. The ewes are only brought in if there is a problem at lambing; last year that meant that just five or six ewes were ever brought in at all. They lamb about 150–160%. There is an odd problem with foxes occasionally taking lambs, but it takes a brave or desperate fox to try and take a lamb from one of these sheep!

In the worst weather, Neville feeds hay. He puts Rumivite blocks out from a couple of weeks before tupping to the 10th of February, then he feeds at about 1lb of 18% protein cake a head, per day until lambing. All the sheep looked very fit the day we visited and it had been very poor weather for a month!

Here he is, bred by Paul Thorp, winner of the Ken Wild Memorial Trophy for James Gill, bought by Neville Belfield for a breed record, and master of all he surveys!

A few Woodies sneak some hay, while they think that we're not looking.

6. THE CHRISTMAS HILL FLOCK

WOODLANDS IN THE EASTERN COUNTIES

There was a light dusting of snow in the crystal clear air of dawn as Katie and I made our way south through the flat lands of Lincolnshire on our way to visit a couple of Woody keepers in Norfolk and Suffolk.

As the miles tumbled past, I was reminded of the trip James and I had taken to Northern Ireland. The potato harvest had been in full flow then, and when we got to some corners or cross roads we would see a few potatoes left at the roadside that had fallen from passing trailers. James and I had decided that this was clear evidence of the great annual potato migration!

In this part of the world in late January it's not potatoes, but sugar beet that was being harvested; but try as I could, I could not convince Katie that there was a sugar beet migration happening!

So, we stopped for coffee on a layby full of beet wagon drivers. Across the flat landscape we could see the billowing chimney of the sugar factory in the distance. The coffee was really bitter. Katie took a sip and with a shudder gazed longingly at the distant white cloud, 'Do you think they'd let us buy just one spoonful of sugar?' she asked with a giggle.

These fen lands are not the natural habitat of sheep. A Woody could walk for miles down here and only have to slow down for the wide, straight dykes and to munch on the fields of vegetables.

We passed one field, however, surrounded by huge fields of leeks and the remnants of Brussels sprout plants, with a feeble-looking electric fence and several hundred Suffolk fat lambs, finishing on what looked like turnips from a distance.

South of Kings Lynn, trees began to fill the landscape, and the country started to roll again. With this change in the landscape, we started to see livestock appear again, along with tiny Muntjac deer. We passed one at the roadside between the woodland and a road sign, and at first I thought it was a little escaped goat. Then I realised what it was and told Katie.

'Oh Dad!' she said knowingly. 'You don't expect me to believe that that was a deer do you?' she asked, in disbelief after the talk of a sugar beet migration. 'It looks more like a big rabbit or something!'

(Actually she used to have some giant rabbits that in a straight fight would probably whip a Muntjac!)

Soon we arrived at Jo and Mike Taylor's Christmas Hill Farm. Jo and Mike are really living the dream; well, my dream anyway!

In 2006 they sold their flocks of sheep and herds of cattle to Mr. and Mrs. R. and P. Baker, the owners of Christmas Hill. The Bakers then employed the Taylors to manage their 700-acre farm for them, investing heavily in miles of new fences and lovely big new buildings!(If there are any rich landowners out there who would like to buy me out and then pay me to run their farm for them, please contact me.)But seriously, Jo and Mike have obviously worked very hard to set up a very productive and well-organised commercial rare breeds unit and Mr. and Mrs. Baker have obviously chosen wisely in selecting the Taylors to manage the farm for them.

Christmas Hill is not an open farm. It is a genuine lamb and beef unit that sells much of its produce through the farm shop, where a full-time butcher is employed. So, Jo is managing all the stock with clear commercial carcass quality at the front of her mind; this is reflected in the quality of livestock on show.

PROFILE - THE CHRISTMAS HILL FLOCK

Flock prefix: Christmashill

Year pedigree flock formed:
1991 (current location from 2006)

Size of pedigree flock: Large (51-100)

Name of breeder: Jo Taylor

Address:
Christmas Hill Farm
Lakenheath, Brandon
Suffolk

Telephone: 07733 258494

Date of profile: 30th January 2010

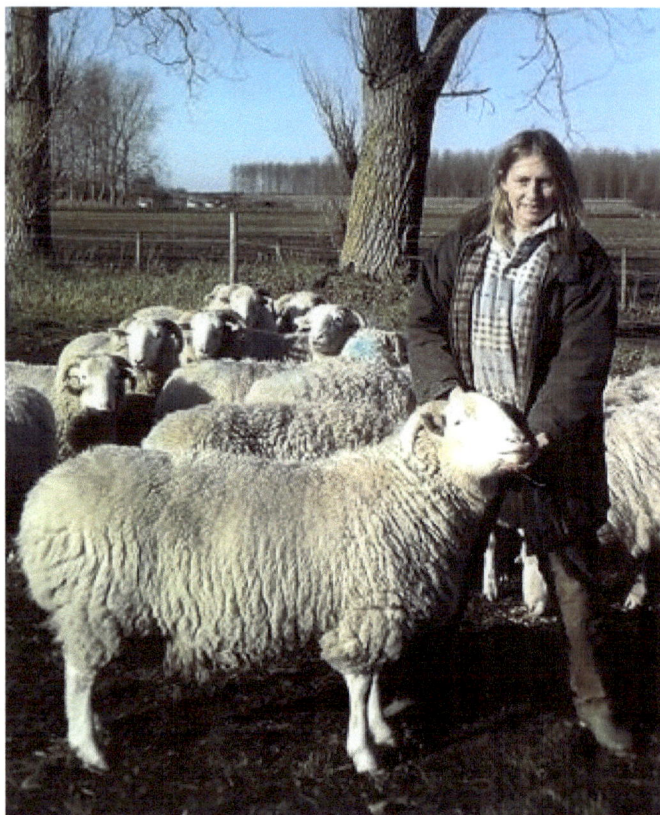

Jo Taylor and one of her ewes

Jo and Mike Taylor have dedicated their lives to proving that there is a place in modern agriculture for rare breeds. Talking to Jo, it soon felt to me that if she were a stick of Blackpool Rock the words 'rare breeds' would be etched through her very core!

Breeding Policy

The flock started as the Fuglemere flock in Buckinghamshire in 1991-92 with two ewes from the Aldenham flock owned by Hertfordshire County Council. They soon built up a flock of 'show quality' sheep from the 'founder ram' from Kent Langholme Aeirlee. I asked Jo what she thinks makes a good show quality Woodland. She tells me that she is looking for a square sheep that has plenty of length, good bone quality and size. She says that they must not be up or down on their pasterns (back legs). She also wants sheep with a flat back.

In the ewe, Jo wants a sheep of basically the 'same type'; it must have a broad face, but not narrow, and the ewe must look feminine. She is trying to get rid of colour around the eyes and spots from the face. Apparently every now and then they get lambs with a few black spots, which while a feature of the Whitefaced Woodland, is something that she is trying to breed out. Jo has found that heavier bodied sheep in her flock tend to be leggy, with wider spaced horns. So, to counter this influence, she has used a heavier ram for a few years, rather than a leggier one, to bring back size; this she feels has led to a more uniform flock.

A Christmas Hill ram

Now they are working on bringing the average age of the ewe flock down, clearing out some of the older ewes that they had that had reached the ages of twelve or thirteen. They haven't bought in any ewes for some years, but if they did, they would not buy ewes with speckles, flyaway horns or horns that are too tight to the face.

Jo has a theory that: 'If a sheep on the hill had horns that were too tight to the face, he'd be dead; therefore Woodlands with tight horns are not suitable for the job.'

So in the ram, Jo will not consider a male to breed from that has horns that need to be slabbed; this she believes would be too much trouble for most hill farmers.

Christmashill Erica, one of the ewe lambs

Farm Details

Year started to farm here: 2006
Size of farm: Group D (101 - 500 ha)
Land classification: Low Land
Farm type: Beef and sheep
Other crops: All grass land
Other breeds of livestock kept: Cattle: Long Horn, South Devon and Belted Galloway.
Sheep: Portland and Hampshire Down

Farm Description

Christmas Hill Farm is a flat lowland farm, sheltered from the worst of the prevailing winds by plantations of trees. The soil is Breckland Sand and Fenland Peat. It is all down to grass and part of the farm floods in winter because it is made up of Water Meadows. Nearby there is a RSPB bird sanctuary and the farm is teaming with wildlife.

Flock Management

The wet soil is deficient in cobalt; this leads to pneumonia-like symptoms, apparently, and a general lack of vigour, especially in the finishing lambs, although it was less noticeable in the Woodies than in the other sheep. They drench the lambs with white wormers containing a cobalt supplement and leave out mineral nutrient supplement licks all winter and salt licks with extra minerals all year round. Ewe pencils are fed four weeks prior to lambing, with haylage fed to supplement the grass when the ewes are confined in smaller fields by very wet ground, as they have been this year.

They lamb inside in a brand-new, purpose-built building. I had asked if they have a fox problem, and sure enough as we return through the buildings, we see a big dog fox leave the open-sided sheds and calmly make his way through the midden back to the fields.

This cocky devil was clearly a town fox, because he showed no respect or fear to us!

Marketing

Woodland lamb is sold through the farm shop, which is a relatively new enterprise and sales have been slow, but are steadily building up. Jo also sells her prize-winning pedigree stock through the Whitefaced Woodland Sheep Society newsletter and on their website, and regularly supplies to established customers such as County Council City Farms in the South East.

7. THE BYWAY FLOCK

We left Christmas Hill Farm and headed into Norfolk to see Chris Steel's flock. Church Farm is set back off a quiet country lane, in a landscape that is almost flat and is dominated by arable farming. At the end of the drive up to the farm we were met by the familiar white faces that we were looking for in an area that had few sheep. My overwhelming memory of the visit was of Chris calmly and resolutely standing holding a Woody ewe as chaos broke all around – Marilyn, Chris's partner was trying to get hold of a sheep using a bucket of cake, while two of his children were also trying to get hold of a sheep a piece to get their pictures taken, and a horde of sheep were all fighting to get to the same bucket! Katie and I must have taken a dozen pictures each, as we tried to get everything and everyone in and looking our way, but it seemed impossible, yet in every picture, Chris is standing there, resolute, like a lighthouse in a turbulent storm-tossed ocean!

As we had entered the wind blasted field, the bitter gale straight off the North Sea had cut through us like a knife, and Chris enquired innocently if I could answer a question for him. I said I'd give it a go, but was no expert.

When I try to sell my sheep up North,' he said, 'they all turn their noses up at these "soft southern sheep"; so tell me Philip, if a sheep can survive in these winds, doesn't that make it hardy?'

Through my chattering teeth, I had to admit that he had a point. It was only later when I got home that it dawned on me: my sheep don't seem to mind the cold, crisp mornings, with a biting wind, it's cold wet weather that kills them! Perhaps Neville Belfield had a point when he said that 'you wouldn't like it if someone put a cut up the back of your jacket on a cold wet day, so I don't like sheep whose jackets have a cut up their backs either!'

So, in answer to your question, Chris, perhaps it takes different types of sheep to do well in different climates, because although I agree that Norfolk can be very cold when the wind blows in off the North Sea, it is perhaps a dryer wind than those they get in the Pennines or Lake District.

PROFILE - THE BYWAY FLOCK

Flock prefix: Byway
Name of breeder: Chris Steel
Address: Church Farm, Long Lane, Banham, Norfolk NR12 2DF
Telephone: 07748 523855
Date of profile: 30th January 2010

Breeding Policy

Chris keeps all his ram lambs entire, so that he can pick the best to breed from. This comes at a price, however, as tup lambs do not finish well in autumn or winter, and he still had a large group of shearling rams that he was still trying to finish, in their second winter. Chris is looking for sheep with horns that grow away from the face, adopting a very similar view to Jo Taylor, in that the flock master should not have to keep trimming or slabbing horns. Then in the ram, Marilyn told me, they are looking for a long straight back, broad shoulders, good teeth and good, big testicles. In the ewes they also want a long straight back, broad hips for lambing, no black marks at all, no topknot and no kemp in the wool.

The stock tup put to a few old girls

Marketing Policy

Chris and Marilyn sell meat from their sheep privately and their meat is in high demand; they also sell pedigree stock privately to people looking for pedigree Woodies and have sold sheep through the newsletter.

Showing Achievements

Chris is a very competitive man; one of the attractions for him of keeping pedigree sheep was clearly showing them, and he told me that they had done twelve shows a year for the past few years. He therefore has many successes under his belt. So to narrow it down, I asked what he was most proud of.

'Best in Breed at the Great Yorkshire Show,' he replied immediately. 'I really felt like I had made it when I beat them all on their home ground! Then it was the Reserve Champion Ewe in the Hill Breed Class – I felt that it was quite an achievement, beating all those popular hill breeds like Swaledales with a rare breed ewe!'

But he quickly went on to tell me how proud he is of his daughter Victoria, who had also won the Junior Handler's Cup at the Royal Norfolk and had been presented to the Queen as a result!

Victoria, Champion Young Handler at the Royal Norfolk Show

Farm Details

One of Chris's ewes

Year started to farm here: 1997
Size of farm: Group B (21-50 ha)
Land classification: Low Land
Farm type: Grassland
Other crops: Some poultry
Other breeds of livestock kept:
Sheep: Texels and Lleyn

Farm Description

Church Farm is a family smallholding, on flattish clay soil. The ground is wet but fertile, and there was grass growing in even the coldest part of winter. The smallholding has a variety of small sheds and a couple of big buildings, one for hay and straw and the other for sheep housing. Chris drives a taxi for a living and works some very antisocial hours, so Marilyn is left to deal with their children, dogs and sheep, ducks and chickens in their extended menagerie.

Flock Management

The ewes are mainly being lambed to Lleyn and Texel tups this year inside in the big shed.

8. THE MORTHAM FLOCK

MAY DAY

The 1st of May had arrived at last! Oh how often during the longest and coldest of winters for so many years, I had longed for the month of May to arrive! Lambing was finally fizzling to an end, the wild cherries along the drive had erupted into blossom, the grass in the meadows was starting to get away and the buds were bursting open on the trees.

So, in the pause before the silage season and shearing starting again, Katie (my daughter) and I arranged a small treat and made a quick visit to Rachel Godschalk's flock to see her new lambs.

Katie and I left the green of Kirkby Lonsdale and headed north up the Lune Valley to Sedbergh and the Howgill Fells beyond. Up in the hills above Kirby Stephen, we were surprised to see that even after a week of temperatures at home in the upper teens (Centigrade) there were still odd patches of snow on the tops. Either that or there were huge piles of wool filling some of the gills, not casualties of four months of snow we hoped!

Passing over the top of the Pennines along the A66, the landscape was still drab and brown too, despite the in-bye land being full of tiny Swale, Dalesbred and Kendal Rough Fell lambs. But as we descended down the other side, we returned to the verdant green of spring once more with lush fields of ankle deep grass and cereals growing between hedges bursting into flower and leaf.

Newly lambed sheep graze the lush new pasture

Rachel farms on the stunning banks of the rivers Tees and Greta in rich, fertile parkland full of spectacular mature trees and two grand country houses. Her charming cottage nestles at the end of a private lane, sheltered by woodland overlooking the Tees itself, and from her windows she can watch, and be watched by, some of her and her mother Ann's Woodies contentedly munching on herb rich meadows full of lesser celandine and clover.

Oh how jealous my own Woodies would have been, if they could have observed how the other half live from their tightly cropped and over-grazed rush pasture on the edge of Docker Moor I thought; but first appearances can be deceptive and we were soon to learn that this lush pasture had only very recently come into Rachel's possession and that the rest of her land had yet to recover from the harsh rigours of winter just like ours.

It would have been interesting to see Rachel's flock just because of the active roles that she and her mother take within the society, but on top of this Rachel has built up one of the largest flocks of Woodlands that I know about, enthusiastically buying in sheep from a great many sources. This has ensured that her flock is possibly one of the most representative of the whole breed – it is certainly the biggest and possibly most genetically diverse one that I have yet seen –

however I was really surprised by the uniformity within it. Such uniformity can only be the result of careful selection. Clearly Rachel has worked hard to find sheep from a variety of sources that fulfil her criteria. This demonstrates a deep knowledge and understanding of the breed, underpinning her enthusiasm for it.

PROFILE - THE MORTHAM FLOCK

Flock prefix: Mortham
Year started farming / pedigree flock formed: 1998
Size of pedigree flock: Major (101+)

Name of breeders: Rachel and Ann Godschalk
Address: North Park Cottage, Rokeby, Barnard Castle DL12 9RZ
Telephone: 01833 627102 / 07962 152242
email: rachelgodschalk@whitefacedwoodland.co.uk

Date of profile: 1st May 2010

Some of Rachel and Ann's ewes

Breeding Policy

Ann originally started the flock with some sheep that she purchased from Chris Steel's flock. Rachel has however built upon this nucleus by selecting sheep that she liked from many others.

Rachel's policy for breeding is a process of elimination; any ewe that has a 'fault' is not bred pure, but put onto her Texel cross Beltex tup. Then, the best 60 of her ewes were put to AI this year, using tups from Paul Thorp, James Gill and Crosshill Keith, from Richard and Sue

Bottom. These ewes were selected as if for showing. Rachel did not want any sheep with tufts on their heads or woolly legs; they have to be 'clean'. She wants the sheep to have a good straight back, to stand well and be good-boned.

A gimmer with a good 'tight' coat and 'flat' horns from the top of the head

All the time she is looking at the legs of her sheep, judging whether the legs are too close, turned in or out, down at the pasterns and so on. She is also looking at the horns. Rachel explained that she wants the horns to be flat; this means flat from the top of the head, not flat in profile or flat to the face.

'It is less important where the horns grow to. I'm not so worried if they end up sticking out a bit,' she said. 'But when the lamb is born, the horns must be growing flat from the top of the head or you can have terrible problems lambing them. You don't want great big horn buds pointing out at horrible angles and ripping the ewe up inside or even getting stuck!'

Rachel also prefers Woodies with wider faces and broader noses, but did not feel that this would be too much of a problem at lambing.

Finally, Rachel will not cull any ewes just because they have one of the faults described above, only if their performance as a mother is poor. Her rejects go to be crossbred, because an animal that would be poor in the show ring might still make an excellent and productive mother. Only sheep that are poor mothers are sent for culling – a policy that will ensure the long-term instinct of mothering within the breed!

A ewe and lamb from the AI group

Marketing Policy

Fat lambs and those not intended for breeding go through the local mart. Rachel takes a number of fat lambs to a local butcher's firm that she knows; he cuts and packs the meat for her very professionally. She sells these directly herself. When Ann started the flock in Hertfordshire, she told me, she used to trade all but one gimmer lamb to a local butcher in exchange for meat credits. This would be a useful model for new comers to sheep-keeping who just have a few lambs, but more than their own family could take, to get into the whole meat marketing business. It would also help to remind the would-be flock master what the true end product of their business is!

Left: Ann holding one of the lambs from the AI group
Right: Rachel shows how the horns of this ewe are flat from the top of the head; the ewe also shows a broad head.

Showing Achievements

When we arrived, Rachel's living room was full of rosettes and trophies. But when asked what their showing achievements were, Rachel modestly told me 'Oh nothing really'.

'So what are all these?' I asked.

'Well I don't think that it means much if you came first when there was little competition. I think that it means more when you measure yourself against real opposition. So, I suppose the ones that I am most proud of are third at the Hope show and a couple of seconds at the Great Yorkshire Show.'

Farm Details

Year started to farm here: 2006
Size of farm: Group C (51 - 100 ha)
Land classification: Non-LFA
Other breeds of livestock kept: Sheep: Texel x Beltex, Welsh Badger-face

Farm Description

Rachel rents land on the banks of the rivers Tees and Greta. It is rich, fairly flat parkland with a series of steep terrace-like banks that must have once been the banks of the river as it cut down from the moors above through this fertile landscape. The ancient pastures are rich in broadleaf herbs and wild flowers.

The landlords keep a few ducks, chickens and geese, which have the run of the courtyard, where Rachel can use some of the buildings, and they also have their own private pond. The landlords also keep a couple of Kerry heifers and a number of Alpacas.

9. THE WOODHEAD FLOCK

BACK TO THE BREED'S ROOTS

Pikenaze Farm

Whenever I read about the Whitefaced Woodland, I encounter the same place names mentioned, Penistone, Glossop, Hope and the Woodlands district of Derbyshire.

When I have travelled through this area while researching the breed, I have to say that I have been disappointed by the scarcity of Whitefaced Woodland sheep; but in a few places, dedicated enthusiasts tenaciously fight against the relentless tide of modern sheep farming fashions to keep alive this rare breed. Jeff Dowey, his wife Helen and their daughter Karen are one such family. Helen is the daughter of the legendary Rider Howard and granddaughter of Arthur Howard, who I have come to view as the 'father' of the modern breed.

Helen and Jeff have now taken over the Pikenaze Farm that for years now I have been reading about (pronounced Pike-naze and not Pic-a-neese as I have always stupidly thought it to be). Karen, their daughter, is now proudly carrying on her family's noble tradition. And here I was driving up the steep track to the farm!

So much of what I have read about the Whitefaced Woodland and so much of what I know about the breed is etched on this hillside. The breed itself has been forged by the conditions found in these hills, and in their turn the sheep and their flock masters have influenced the very appearance of this landscape.

The Woodland (Jeff firmly corrects my incorrect use of the word 'Woody') is classed as a hill breed and this is a hill farm!

Pikenaze Farm clings to the edge of the steep hillside, with towering hills and moors all around it, and on the last day of July in 2010 the dried up Woodhead Reservoir below. It was a cold day for July and the wind being funnelled up the steep-sided valleys was full of sharp, cutting rain showers. It felt more like the middle of winter than the middle of summer, and I really sympathised with the newly shorn sheep.

Sheep and their shepherds have to be hard to survive here. The harsh realities of life up here make certain that only the very fittest can survive! If sheep can survive here, then they will thrive anywhere! And here they were, perhaps not the biggest Whitefaced Woodlands that I had ever seen, but great, solid, strapping sheep with broad faces and strong bones, Derbyshire's finest breed in their home territory!

PROFILE - THE WOODHEAD FLOCK

Year started farming: 1987
Year pedigree flock formed: 1990
Size of pedigree flock: Major (101+)

Name of breeders: Karen and Jeff Dowey
Address: Pikenaze Farm, Woodhead, Glossop, Derbyshire
Telephone: 01457 861577/ 07931 143287(Jeff) / 07787 241960(Karen)
email: karendowey@whitefacedwoodland.co.uk

Date of profile: 31ˢᵗ July 2010

Flock History

My research shows that Woodlands have been bred in this area for hundreds of years, certainly since long before the current roads, walls and fences have been constructed; although it is probable that Roman road that passes through Pikenaze Farm actually predates the breed.

Moreton Thomas writing in *Livestock Heritage*, a RBST publication of 1981, tells us that according to Arthur Howard, when the reservoirs were first built in Derbyshire they flooded the precious in-bye land of local farms and just after they were built sheep were removed from the surrounding hills, as it was thought that they would pollute this precious drinking water resource. But this proved to be a mistake, and rank weed growth blocked the watercourses and water stagnated in the wet ground above causing pollution, and so sheep were reintroduced to area.

The Woodlands returned to their home range, but this did not last for long, Thomas tells us, because during the hard times of the thirties and forties the Woodlands' larger carcass gave it a 'special sanction for slaughter'.

Arthur Howard, Karen's great grandfather, came to Pikenaze Farm in 1942, having sold his chicken farm to finance the move. During the War, lamb, mutton and chicken were highly valued products for a country cut off from its empire by German U-boats and enduring harsh rationing.

The severe blizzards of 1947 further reduced the breed to two or three flocks. One of which was at Pikenaze Farm, first under Arthur Howard and then under his son Rider Howard.

Jeff Dowey married Helen, Rider's daughter, in 1987 and the couple have taken over the tenancy of the farm now. Jeff told me that his own interest in the breed was really reinvigorated when Karen, their daughter, started to take a keen interest in showing and breeding the Woodland, and they took over the current flock in 1990, selected from the stock of Woodlands at Pikenaze.

Rider Howard keeps on the Pikenaze flock name himself, which has now moved with him, and, while it can't be argued that his influence isn't still here, he has gracefully stepped back to allow his granddaughter to make her own mark on her flock; although he has given her some excellent sheep. The family are quite competitive, but I am sure that Rider would have been proud to be beaten by his granddaughter at this year's Great Yorkshire Show with her gimmer lamb.

Breeding Policy

Jeff assessing a group of sheep

Karen and Jeff are very critical of all their own sheep as they go about the daily task of running a large hill farm. They consider the head, bone, jacket, feet, faces, eyes and pasterns of all the animals in their care, constantly striving to perfect and refine the breeding of their best Woodlands.

They operate a ruthless cull policy, inherited from Rider. If an animal is not up to the task, it must be culled, in an insatiable quest for perfection.

Above all Karen and Jeff want power and size in their sheep, it is only then that they start down the list of other features listed above

The flock lambs in April and May outside on the lower slopes of the hill. In the main lambing fields they have erected some shelters from the biting wind that screams up the Woodhead pass, using some curved corrugated sheets as windbreaks, held by fencing stakes on their sides for lambs to shelter behind.

Behind this ewe you can see three of the windbreak shelters for lambing sheep

Jeff told me an interesting fact that might be of great relevance to all of us: 'Some of our best stock getting tups are sawn horned tups.'

Jeff pointed out that you could always saw the horns if they threaten to cut into a tup's face. It's a shame to waste a good powerful tup like the one below, just because his horns are tight. What is more to the point is that some of these big powerful tups need their horns to be sawn off.

Rider Howard bred this tup, note the big broad head, strong body and closeness of the horns

53

Karen with one of her tups

As we travelled around the farm looking at all the other sheep, those not destined for showing necessarily still had the same broad faces. A typical Woodhead Woodland would have a broad forehead, a modest Roman nose and horns that were well set back out the back of the head.

All pure male Woodland lambs are kept entire from birth. Jeff and Karen then start to weed out any lambs displaying any noticeable faults at weaning. Like all the best breeders they are very critical of their own flock, constantly looking to refine and perfect their breeding stock, and sending the rest as fat lambs. Lambs that are too small for the fat trade or which might be worth keeping for breeding are wintered on dairy farms lower down the valley.

'Some years we've kept no tups back at all!' Jeff proudly tells us. This policy is one that many newcomers to sheep breeding would do well to learn from!

Marketing Policy

All sheep not wanted for breeding purposes are sold through Welsh Country Foods, who send a representative to the farm to grade lambs for slaughter on a regular basis.

'He'll take everything, and we have difficulty stopping him from taking the lambs that we want to keep sometimes!' Jeff said. 'All he is interested in is whether it is fat enough and will meet their requirements!'

Showing Achievements

'This year I beat my granddad!' Karen jumps in with straight away, obviously a big achievement in her eyes, and I can't say I blame her. I'd love to produce a sheep of any description that would be anything near as good as one of Rider Howard's!

Karen has had huge success at the Great Yorkshire, winning a first for a shearling ewe in 2007, the trophy for 'Wool on the Hoof' in 2008, sweeping the board with six firsts and six seconds in 2009 and this year with her gimmer lamb beating her grandfather! (Rider has asked me to point out that he didn't show any sheep in 2009!)

Now Karen has her eye fixed on Hayfield and Hope shows. 'Because Grandad's won those and I want my name on the cup too!' she says with a beam! Poor Rider!

The show team line up

Farm Details

Year farm started: 1942
Size of farm: Group F (1000+ ha)
Land classification: LFA, SDA
Farm type: Sheep and beef
Other crops: None
Other breeds of livestock kept:
Cattle: Limousin X and Blue Greys
Sheep: Rough Fell, Swaledale, Dalesbred, Scottish Blackface, Lonk, Gritstone, Herdwick, Texel, Bluefaced Leicesters, Torwen (white bellied) and Torddu (black bellied) – versions of the Badger Face Welsh Mountain – Lleyn, and some Soay crosses (from the St Kilda archipelago) and a number of crosses.

Flock Management

There are 45 tups in all on the farm (only fifteen of which are Whitefaced Woodlands) for the thousand or so sheep. The ewes lamb in April and May outside. Ewes are wormed at lambing, shearing time and burling time (that is when the tails are clipped before flushing and prior to tupping). All the sheep are in the Heptavac programme. Dipping is carried out as necessary. For the sheep kept in the lower ground – mainly the best show Woodlands – this means dipping in the spring (May) to avoid fly-strike. Those sheep on the higher ground are usually dipped later in the year (July) for fly, ticks and lice. Jeff points out that flies are more of a nuisance around the wooded valley than up on the open hilltop.

Karen shows us Kneel, so called because of his habit of kneeling when they try to get hold of him

All the sheep have access to good quality haylage all winter and get sugar beet nuts for six to eight weeks before lambing.

Fluke is an occasional problem, but not too bad, and only when it is a particularly wet year.

Foxes and other predators are a constant problem, especially at lambing time.

Like for the rest of us, there are constant problems with red tape, hikers getting lost or leaving gates open, officials and landlords with unrealistic expect-ations, but they seem to be 'mekin a go of it' as we say up here in Cumbria! I wish I was doin' as well!

10. THE PIKENAZE FLOCK

MEETING THE LEGEND

It is five in the morning, and our house is quiet and peaceful. Everyone else is fast asleep, but my head is spinning with thoughts and images from yesterday; so I am drawn to my computer to write them down while it's all fresh in my mind. I know that everyone who keeps Whitefaced Woodland sheep does so for their own reasons, and that these reasons are different: there are those who want to rescue a rare breed, those that want to show, some who wish to keep alive their local breed and so on. But when most people start to become interested in a breed, they want to find out more about that breed and for me personally, that line of enquiry has become a dominant force in my life. I have never shown sheep at an agricultural show and don't particularly want to; but I enjoy seeing them and learning about them and their owners.

For anyone who has kept Whitefaced Woodlands in any kind of a serious way, there is one name with which you will be familiar, one man and his family who dominated the history of the breed in the twentieth century and will continue to do so well into the twenty-first century. This gentleman has become something of a legend. Appearing almost magically from the background, he sweeps the prizes in the showing ring, then vanishes back to the hills. Everyone who keeps Woodland sheep has sheep that are related in some way to his flock, but you can't buy any of his stock these days. All the top breeders claim their best sheep come from his bloodlines, but these are no longer available. Everyone in the Woodland world that I talk to, know about his sheep, but very few get to see them, except those he presents in the show ring. Everyone tells you that yes, they know where he farms, but no one is quite sure where it is, except those chosen few. This is because this is a gentleman who guards his privacy and his sheep very closely, and so, for me, it was the greatest of honours to be granted the privilege of visiting his farm with my children, and to be allowed to take as many pictures as we liked. Furthermore, I'll share some of them with you here today, but with this privilege comes a grave responsibility, because I've nothing but respect for the lifetime of work that has gone into building this irreplaceable flock, and I realise that I can't do anything that might jeopardise what is truly a hidden gem, and hidden it must remain in this greedy, selfish world.

This then, ladies and gentlemen is the flock profile for Mr. Rider Howard.

PROFILE - THE PIKENAZE FLOCK

Year flock established: 1942
Size of pedigree flock: Major (101+)

Name of breeders: Rider Howard
Address: in the Peak District (please make any contact through the author)
Date of profile: 20th November 2010

Rider Howard watches over one of his giant tups

Flock History

Arthur Howard, Rider's father, started the flock at Pikenaze Farm, Woodhead in 1942, and Rider passed Pikenaze Farm on to his daughter Helen and her husband Jeff in 1986 when he bought his current farm, but he kept the Pikenaze flock name. These sheep are descended then from the few flocks of sheep kept by Arthur Howard (Rider's father) and his neighbours. It is a closed flock, with very few sheep being brought into it in the past decades. The simple truth is that there are no other flocks that could fully replace these bloodlines if they were to be lost.

The history of this flock is the history of the Whitefaced Woodland breed.

Breeding Policy

Rider Howard's breeding policy is summed up beautifully in one simple sentence, 'You can't breed rats from mice!'

But do not let this fool you; there is nothing simple about the breeding of these huge sheep! There is not a single detail of his sheep that he does not consider very carefully indeed. But even a novice like me can see that in the Pikenaze flock, size matters above all else. Rider breeds big-boned, powerful sheep with broad shoulders, great length and legs planted like telegraph poles, firmly at the four corners of their bodies. Their horns come tightly from the backs of their heads, down close to their faces, and if they get too close in his tups, they're sawn off; it's that simple. Indeed, many of his best tups have had their horns sawn off. These sheep have broad faces and strong Roman noses.

Rider, as with all the most knowledgeable breeders that I have spoken to, has noticed that pure white Woodlands with pink noses and pink feet are slightly more susceptible to foot rot, so he doesn't care too much for this passion that some have for breeding pure white, pink nosed Woodlands; he doesn't seem overly concerned by what he describes as blue-nosed sheep. Actually he proudly points out one tup to me with a few dark speckles on his muzzle that is otherwise an outstanding tup. Okay, this tup might not be rated top in the show ring, but personally I would say that it beats most that I've seen! A few blackish specks don't detract from what is otherwise an outstanding tup. Nevertheless, this tup is relegated to the second division in Rider's flock, because there are better tups!

The same is also true of the tuft of wool on the forehead of one of the ewes in the flock of his best sheep. Some breeders that I've spoken to are almost obsessed with weeding out this 'fault', but although I could only see one or two ewes in his flock displaying this tuft, it doesn't seem to worry Rider. He is looking at the shape, size, conformation and power of his sheep first. Perhaps there is a lesson here for all of us, with so many variables to worry about, perhaps we would be better off concentrating on getting one thing right – good, big, healthy sheep! So what if they have a black spot on their nose or a tuft on their head…they must have size, bone, and broad, straight backs first.

'You can't breed rats from mice!'

Note the strength of bone in this ewe

Marketing Policy

It is no coincidence that the more successful flocks share one very important tool in their formation – a strong cull policy. In my humble opinion, Rider Howard's flock is so exceptional because he operates such a precise cull policy. Everything that fails to meet his high standards for breeding from is sent 'off down the road'. Rider started the farm with a green field site and has reorganised the fields to all lead into a set of superb sheep pens, now enclosed from the weather in their own dedicated building. Here sheep can be sent effortlessly through a shedding race, where a rep from a large national meat marketing company can cut off all the best fat lambs that he wants into a large pen for loading onto a wagon for the trip to the slaughterhouse. It is all very organised and extremely efficient. Judging by the well-used set up, I expect that lambs will all be used to passing through the yard, and by the time that they are ready to go, they must just think it to be another ordinary day – a stress-free day for all concerned.

A group of massive ewes. Note the strong bone, broad shoulders, and faces.
The tuft on the forehead of one and the blue nose of the other are only minor faults.

The only really shocking part for me was that Rider had marked so few tup lambs to keep, when there were so many good ones to choose from! (They had used some cheap pig branding and it had run in the rain, so there was no doubting which were to be kept.)

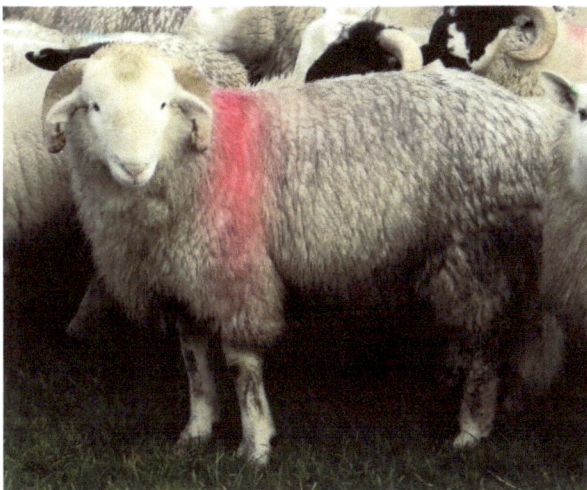

The tup lamb on the left is marked to keep, the other isn't.
Rider said that the tuft on the first would be lost as he matures.

'Oh well,' he said almost reluctantly as we looked at one fantastic tup lamb that wasn't marked to keep. 'I suppose I ought to keep that one. But the thing is that he has only come on since I put him in here on corn, to fatten. You can't always tell when you first bring them in that they are going to make decent tups. And some you think will make good tups, don't make the grade after all.'

So he's flexible as well; another lesson that we could all learn from!

Showing Achievements

Perhaps it would be easier to say what Rider hasn't won, as he has been setting the bar in this area for years, winning at the Great Yorkshire many times. But I'm not sure if he will ever win the Ken Wild Trophy at Bretton Mill in the future, because you have to be prepared to sell your best tups to do that and he doesn't seem to want to do so. Perhaps if he did, we would see the record for the highest price paid for a Woodland pass the two thousand pound mark!

Farm Details

Year started here: 1987
Size of farm: Group D (101-500 ha)
Land classification:, SDA, LFA
Farm type: Sheep
Other crops or livestock: None

This photograph does not do justice to the size of these ewes, because the tup is so huge.

Farm Description

Rider Howard farms at over 900 feet high, on land reclaimed from heather moorland, but despite this it is surprisingly flat land with a rich, black, peaty soil. When he took over the land it was mainly thick, coarse Molinia grass (the purple moor grass is only found on very acid, wet soils), but careful management using tight grazing cattle and sheep, some reseeding and selective feeding with hay has improved the land considerably on what is just up the road. Careful planting with shelterbelts and the restoration of high dry-stone walls has improved the shelter from the prevailing winds dramatically.

I have already described the efficient layout of sheep handling pens, but these are just a small detail in the well-thought-out layout of all the new buildings that he has erected since taking over the land. Rainwater is harvested from the sheds to supplement the mains supply and help reduce costs. In a dry summer like the one that has just past, there is a shortage of water on the farm and this has to be managed very carefully.

When he took over the farm, there weren't enough internal boundaries, but Rider has turned this into an advantage by setting out a field network that effortlessly feeds gathered livestock into the central yard in front of the new buildings.

The layout of the farm includes a couple of very well protected paddocks next to the building to accommodate any sick animals or those which require an extra bit of care and attention. The now redundant cattle shed has also been converted into the same use, when not being used to house sheep with adopted lambs, or any of the many other uses that a good shepherd has to put such accommodation to. It also houses a cosy brew house for the workers and passing roving reporters and their offspring.

Another giant tup standing head and shoulders above a group of shearlings. To give you some idea of his size, the wall is over five feet tall! These shearling ewes are bigger than most sheep that I've seen, of any breed!

Flock Management

Despite his excellent new buildings, there simply isn't enough room to lamb all his sheep inside, and is that necessary when you keep breeds like the Whitefaced Woodland anyway? So the sheep lamb outside in late-April and May. Because the sheep lamb outside, it is important that the breeding stock all have backwards facing horns that come out tight to the head at lambing, otherwise both ewe and lamb would probably die if the horn buds got stuck in the ewe's pelvis.

The lambs are weaned in September and ewes are flushed pre-tupping after being wormed and fluked. The ewes were wormed with Ivomectin wormers, which would also take care of any scab mites if these were present (there absolutely didn't appear to be any such problem there when I visited, I hasten to add).

Many of the Woodlands are kept for most of the year on the heather moor, and were only down on the meadows for tupping time. This makes their fleeces characteristically grey. Some of these hefted ewes were included in the flocks run with Rider's best tups as he works to improve the quality of all his sheep.

Fat lambs are fed ad-lib creep, which he calls corn (we call it provin up here), from hoppers scattered about the fattening fields. I have never seen so many of these in one place!

Hay is mainly bought in, but Jeff, Rider's son in law, round bales some haylage for him too from a few better meadows. Judging from the quantities of forage that he has, and the length of grass that he still had in November, I would say that his stocking rates must be quite extensive over the winter, with forage being used to supplement the diets mainly in the most severe of weather.

The acid nature of the soil means that Rider has to supplement the ewes' diet with copper boluses to avoid swayback problems. We have to do the same; it is not uncommon on acid soils.

11. THE HIGH MOSS FLOCK

STOTT HALL

Jill Falkingham and Paul Thorp have one of the most influential and important Whitefaced Woodland flocks around. There are few farms that I know of that have more Woodlands, and their constant search for perfection has taken them to the top in the show ring on many occasions.

Many of the top Woodland breeders have tups from Paul's flock and I would like to remind readers that Paul bred the record breaking tup that started these flock profiles off.

These flock profiles are not just about the sheep; they are also an opportunity to put the whole farm into context and learn something about the conditions that these sheep are reared under and also about the people behind the flock too. So it is important to say that there can be very few flocks of any breed of sheep that are kept at such a high altitude and in such harsh conditions in England today. So these sheep aren't just well bred, they are hardy too.

This then is their flock profile.

PROFILE - THE HIGH MOSS FLOCK

Year started farming: mid-1990s

Year flock established: 2004

Size of Woodland flock: Major (101+)

Name of breeders: Jill Falkingham and Paul Thorp

Address: Stott Hall, Rishworth,
Sowerby Bridge HX6 4QY

Telephone:
01422 823666
07712 232087(Paul)
07730 402812(Jill)
email: jillyf1@fsmail.net

Date of profile: 28th November 2011

Flock History

Paul originally went to work part time for Ken Wild and part time for Rider Howard. When Mr. Wild passed away, Paul managed to secure the tenancy of Stott Hall from Yorkshire Water. He took over Mr. Wild's famous flock of Whitefaced Woodlands and was fortunate enough to get at least one tup from Rider Howard as well, amongst others.

Since then he has built up one of the biggest Whitefaced Woodland flocks in the country, and today has around 500 Whitefaced Woodland and Woodland crosses, as well as a show flock that he keeps on his family's land at Wild Boar Clough Farm, Hade Edge. This farm is still over 1000ft high and the tups come to Stott Farm for tupping; so even the show sheep are hardy hill sheep.

It's a hard life farming up on these moors and Paul and Jill see showing sheep as one of their main interests. So, with bloodlines that go back to two of the most influential flocks in the country, they are well placed to breed some of the best Whitefaced Woodlands sheep around, including the tup that still holds the record to this day for the highest price ever paid for a Whitefaced Woodland.

Breeding Policy

'Living up here, I think one of the most important things a sheep should have is a good jacket,' Paul explained. It is important that we define exactly what he means, so for a while we discussed this subject in detail. What Paul is looking for is a tight, dense fleece that remains closed in high winds and sheds water easily.

He shyly admits that he doesn't mind a bit of kemp (that's the coarse, hair-like wool), because it stands up well to the elements. This kemp often makes a sheep hardier, and is what Herdwick breeders in the lakes have focused upon in making that breed particularly hardy. Of course, wool manufacturers do not like kemp, and so kempy fleeces are often much lower in value off the sheep. But what good is that if the sheep is dead through hypothermia?

He then told me that the mouth is also important. We all know this; everything follows the mouth! So a sheep with a poor mouth will never do as well as a sheep with a good correct mouth.

Then Paul looks at the bone (legs and feet!)

'They have to be straight with some good strong bone – not too thick set as some people like, but not spindly and narrow either, just enough to support a big strong sheep.'

Jill is really into showing sheep too. Apparently the two of them spend some time discussing the merits of sheep as they fit them into their breeding programme.

'We'll both stand back and take a good hard look at the whole sheep,' Jill explained. 'Paul prefers a tup with a broad masculine head, but I don't mind a sheep with a narrower head.'

'Does size matter?' I ask.

'Well aye, but it's more the length and depth of the sheep that you want,' Paul explained. 'You don't want too much wind under it!'

Beautifully put on a day like this! I immediately get an image of a sheep being blown off the hill onto the M62!

'You don't want one of these sheep that's all leg! You need a good deep body on a ewe.'

Close to the ground, tight fleeced but with a bit of kemp, a typical commercial Stott Hall ewe

A Stott Hall tup

Showing Achievements

Paul's best achievement in the show ring so far was probably with a homebred ewe that came second to the tup he'd also bred, shown and owned by James Gill at the Hope Show 2009. This ewe also went on to win many other prizes for them. The tup, as mentioned before, went on to become Champion of Champions of the breed, and was sold for the breed's record price to Neville Belfield later that year.

Jill is very proud of her two-year-old filly that came second in a huge class of ponies at the Great Yorkshire and their homebred shearling ewe High Moss Zoe also won Overall Breed Champion at the same show

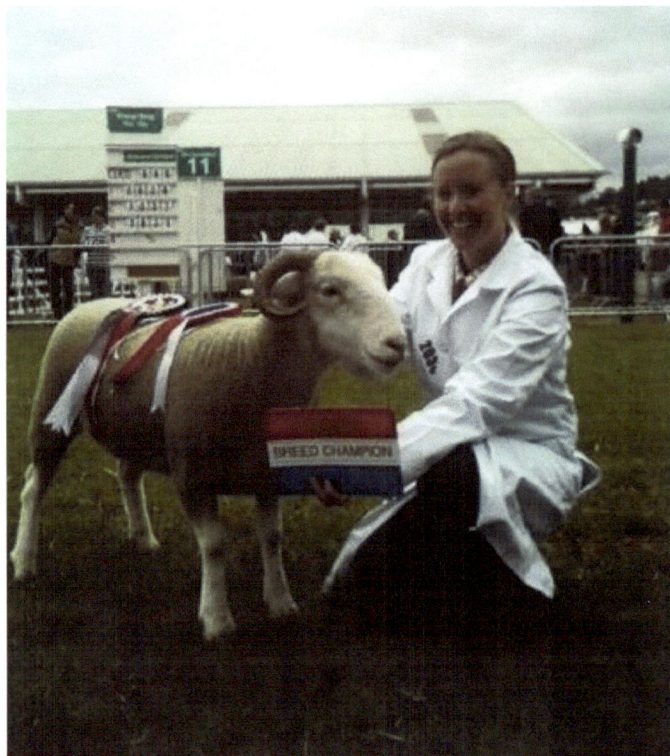

Jill proudly shows her ewe at the Great Yorkshire Show

Farm Details

Year started here: 2004
Size of farm: Group F (1000+ ha)
Land classification:, SDA, LFA
Farm type: Sheep
Livestock: Mainly Woodlands and Woodland crosses, also Swaledales, Gritstones, Lonks, Herdwicks, and Cheviots. Jill also has some Welsh Mountain Ponies.

Farm Description

Stott Hall Farm is classed as a severely disadvantaged hill farm, high in the moors between Manchester and Huddersfield. Thick with rushes and coarse grasses, the land is poor and wet, with many areas of boggy moorland. There are few trees and precious little shelter, except the steep terrain itself and drystone walls.

The valley itself would be a quiet almost tranquil place, were it not for the huge motorway thundering through it. Their in-bye land is mainly just around the motorway itself or down by the huge man-made reservoir below. But even this land is far from flat, and the soil is thin and acidic and full of rock and stone.

Paul and Jill have built a lovely new shed that we had the AGM in, and have another for hay and the buildings attached to the farm itself. To get to the farm one has to go under the motorway itself, and Katie and I thought that the bridge would make a great sheep shed too! Apparently they have used this area to store fertiliser and other essentials, but some passing idiot decided it might be a good idea to set fire to the nitrates! Thank goodness he failed or the whole motorway would have been blown up – although on second thoughts….no don't be silly someone could have been hurt!

Flock Management

The ewes all lamb in May outside. This year they put the tups out on the 26th of November. Normally it is the 28th but they moved it forward slightly to help with their wedding arrangements next year.

They bring the ewes down to the lower fields by the reservoir to lamb. I asked if they have a fox problem, but Paul's brother works very hard on dealing with that problem and is probably helped somewhat by the presence of the motorway through the farm.

They send about 500 sheep away to be wintered on lower ground, and they keep the show flock at the family farm at Hade Edge, so these sheep never go on the moor and as they send many away for the winter, they are able to take sheep off a large part of the moor all winter in compliance with the HLS requirements. The purpose of this is to allow the heather to regenerate and it's early days yet, but Paul says that you can see a bit of a difference already.

During the summer they can only put those 500 sheep on the moor, so even then they are very thinly spread.

When selecting sheep to keep, they have to be hard. Life on the moors isn't easy, so they select them very carefully. A sheep's jacket is a high priority for them here as in breeding.

Sometimes they finish some of their own lambs, but to do so on such thin soils at this altitude can be expensive, so most lambs are sold as stores. This year they had about 120 lambs left when I visited just after Christmas, but it had been a mild autumn and there was plenty of grass about still. These were mainly polled lambs, out of Whitefaced Woodlands, by Texel tups, but they were all away on lower grass keep to fatten. When they bring them back, they may keep some in the shed to fatten, but most will be sent on to finish as stores.

In the last few weeks before lambing, they get the ewes scanned and then they will pull out the geld ewes, but Paul doesn't have enough fields to separate into twins and singles and triplets. This seems ironic with so much land, but the moorland, in particular, tends to be great huge open spaces and dividing a flock of this size up on land like that would be difficult. On top of which is the added problem of the moors now all being open access.

Apparently walkers who left gates open were a minority, but with open access the public just don't get that the sheep are being kept in separate lots and will just leave the gate open for others following in their party and the last through assume the gate was supposed to be open. Apparently mountain bikers are the worst for this. I suppose that stopping and getting off their bikes to shut a gate is too much trouble – so they don't bother!

They also have a problem with dogs being let off their leads. As people come through the gates, they release Fido to run and play, forgetting that genetically Fido is almost identical to his big brother the wolf. Then we get Fido setting off in hunt mode and causing all sorts of problems and damage!

All the sheep are in the Heptavac-P system and they drench for fluke and worms at clipping and before tupping. Because it is a Water Authority owned farm, they are not allowed to dip anymore, and the dip was removed and in exchange they bought them a sheep shower. This is very good for fly control and all the sheep are put through it in the spring, but Paul has concerns that it would not kill scab mites, especially ones hiding in the sheep's ears, so he also injects with dectomax to ensure there is no scab outbreak.

Tups line up

INTERLUDE: HAROLD HODGSON – A LIFE UNDER KINDER

Harold Hodgson (left) pictured with Clive Mitchell and Clive's record-breaking tup

It was a mizzle-filled winter's day in late winter of 2012 when I went to visit Harold and Dorothy in their warm comfortable new home. Harold's eyes twinkled as he recounted tales of farming life from before the War to this day. This then, is an article based on these reminiscences, and it is full of interesting accounts that have great relevance to the history not only of Harold and Dorothy but to the whole of farming in the High Peak during the twentieth century and to the core of the Woodland breed itself.

Harold Hodgson was born in 1929 at Hill House Farm under Kinder Scout. His father had taken on the tenancy of Hill House in 1927, and Harold, in his turn, took over the farm in 1965, where he lived with his sister Dorothy right up until Christmas 2011, when Dorothy's ill health forced them both into a retirement home in Chapel on the Frith.

Hill House Farm (at its peak) had about 176 acres of in-bye land, and they shared the grazing on Kinder with their landlords and another farm. In those days they got up to about 1,100 sheep and a small herd of suckler cows. They mainly kept three breeds of sheep, Lonks, Gritstones and Woodlands. Harold has always kept Woodlands, the local native breed, and he had a flock of about one hundred pure-bred sheep for many years, but this dwindled to about sixty in later years. He became a popular and respected breeder and show judge, and has had a huge influence on other breeders and the breed itself throughout his life.

Before the War, Harold recalled, the moors were mainly kept clear of most sheep. This was because the landlords wanted the land almost exclusively for grouse shooting. But food

Lonk ewes photographed circa 1916. Note tufts on heads

shortage during the War and just after meant that there was a need to repopulate the moors with sheep. Of course, under recent governments the environmental movement is once again moving towards limiting moorland grazing as I pointed out to him.

'Aye,' Harold smiled behind wise, sharp eyes, 'but it'll all happen again! There'll be some other crisis one day and we'll need the food and they'll bring the sheep back to the moors again!'

'We used to keep our sheep out on the hill all year round, only bringing them into the in-bye land for lambing and at tupping time. We had to do that to keep the various breeds apart for tupping, you see. We used to have some of the neighbours' sheep coming over to the sunny side of the hill too. The trouble was they wouldn't go back again!'

Harold thinks it was this drive to clear the moors of sheep that really started the decline of the Woodland. We talked about the history of the breed, and later while discussing the Penistone breed and its relationship with the Woodland (which were once two separate breeds), Harold suddenly came up with a very interesting story, but as it is related to this, I shall recount it here.

'Ah well, that all started back in about 1854 when the breach-loading shotgun came to the fore,' Harold told me. 'The breach-loading shotgun was a lot quicker to load than the muzzle-loaded gun that went before. The moor owners wanted the moors for grouse shooting because now a really good shot could get four birds from one covey as the grouse hurtled over at up to 60 miles an hour, firing first one gun and then getting a loaded gun from his loader. This was much more efficient than the muzzle-loaded gun had ever been, and shooting grouse really took off as a pastime of the upper classes

'So the owners made the tenants take their sheep off the moors, and a lot of sheep from the Woodlands were sent to the annual sheep fair at Penistone, where the locals bought them for themselves. That's where the Penistone came from. It was really a Woodland crossed onto their

Limestone ewe circa 1910

bigger local sheep. The Penistone was a much taller, rougher animal than the Woodland, which were smaller and more meaty – if you know what I mean?'

Perhaps we should mention here that the Lonk and Gritstone breeds are both very closely related to the Woodland too. The Lonk, in particular, is believed to be derived from crossing both the Westmorland Limestone and the Woodland onto the local black-faced heath sheep of Lancashire.

Many writers subscribe to the theory that the Westmorland Limestone was in truth a 'sister' breed to the Woodland, but evidence to support this is hard to come by, as the Limestone died out in 1914 at the start of the First World War. I have long held the view that Limestones from Westmorland may well have been traded south and ended up being crossed with other breeds, and that it was perhaps that through this movement we have had some Limestone genes get into the Woodland. Several writers have over the years talked of the movement south each year of stock from Scotland to Westmorland, from Westmorland to Lancashire and from Lancashire to Cheshire and Derbyshire. Amongst these are Fairy, Holt, Garnett and Ryder.

But there is little hard evidence that Westmorland Limestones were brought to the High Peak. So the hairs on my neck began to stand up when Harold started to tell of how local farmers used to travel every year up to Kirby Steven to buy sheep.

'Had your father always done this?' I asked.

'Oh aye,' he replied as though everyone knew that, 'we always used to go up and buy wether lambs of about a year old and bring them south to fatten them up. And we used to go to Clitheroe in Lancashire every year too.'

Champion Swaledale tup, Kirkby Stephen 1910

This then is an interesting traditional behaviour. Many modern farming practices are deeply rooted in an unwritten traditional history. Of course, Harold's father was not buying Limestones as they were already extinct by his day, and he was buying wethers anyway. But one must ask why? The answer is clear and one many farmers will follow today – they were buying sheep from further up the hill (so to speak) to get hardy animals to bring down to lower levels where they would consequently do well and thrive. So if this farm were doing it with wethers, then other farms would do it with breeding sheep for the same reason.

If the Hodgsons were not buying Westmorland Limestones directly, by going to Clitheroe and buying Lonks, they were definitely bringing in Limestone genes, because the Lonk is a comparatively new breed and, according to Garnett, was developed from the Limestone in the first place. Furthermore, the Limestone was used to improve several breeds local to Kirkby Stephen and the picture above of a Swaledale (another breed heavily influenced by early additions of Limestone blood) shows the typical top knot associated with the Limestone at the time.

'How did you get up there before the War?' I asked.

'Well we used to take a bus into town and then get the train, north,' Harold replied, 'from Hayfield station.'

'Didn't you take the bus all the way to Clitheroe?' Dorothy asked.

'Oh aye, we'd go on the bus to Clitheroe.'

'So how did you get the sheep home?' I asked. 'Not on the same bus?'

Harold laughed. 'Well we wouldn't book a wagon unless we knew we had bought some sheep. We used to fetch sheep back from Clitheroe in a wagon; we'd fetch Woodlands home from Derwent in a cattle-trailer - we had one by the time I took over from my father in 1965 - but we used to fetch sheep home from Kirkby Stephen on the train.

'When we got to Hayfield station, we'd close the gates onto the road and unload the wagons onto the platform. We often had two wagon loads of sheep. The porters used to grumble about all the sheep muck that we'd leave behind on the platform. Then when we had them all unloaded, we'd open the gates onto the road and walk the sheep up the hill the last two miles to the farm.'

'Two miles isn't so far,' I agreed. 'We often walk ours home five miles from Kirkby Lonsdale, but we follow them with a trailer, because you always get one or two go off their legs at some point, don't you? What did you do about that? Follow them with a horse and cart and load them into that?'

'Oh no, we carried sheep shears with us and if a hogg went off its legs we'd shear it there and then, and we'd have a sharp knife too, so we'd trim its feet and then put it over the wall onto the fell. Then we'd roll up the fleece tightly and put a rope around it and carry that home over our backs, and come back for the wether a lot later on, by then it would have filled out a bit on the grass. Sometimes we wouldn't see it again till shearing time when we gathered the fell.

'One year we had a real problem with some hoggs we brought back from the other side of Kinder. I think they had vitamin D deficiency. Anyway, we had a few lie down in the road and go all stiff. So we sheared them and trimmed their feet and put them over the wall onto the fell to grow on. They always did well on the moor. We'd fatten them over the winter and shear them the following summer, and if they still weren't fat enough, then we could turn them out again for another winter and sell them the following year. In those days we'd keep wethers until they had all their teeth, and it wasn't uncommon to keep wethers up to six years.

'To keep the sheep as we turned them onto the fell, we'd punch some holes in a bucket and light a fire in it and heat up a horn iron and horn brand them before we turned them free.'

'What sort of lambs did you buy in Kirkby Stephen?' I asked.

'Well they were mainly Swaledales, some Scotties and a few Herdwicks,' he replied. 'We always had some Woodlands on the farm, but when I took over I set about building up a pure flock. So if anyone was selling some draft ewes I would go along to the sale to check them out. I got my best original stock from Mr. Ollershaw's sale out of Derwent. It was called Ash Farm I think. Then we got some from Mr. Elliot in Derwent too.'

This makes Harold's foundation stock true Woodlands as opposed to Penistones.

'So what were you looking for when you selected Woodlands?'

'Good fleeces,' he replied as all breeders do.

So, as I always have to, I asked what he meant by a good fleece.

'Good quality wool without kemp, either white kemp or black kemp in the breach. As for pink noses, it didn't matter then. As far back as I can remember Woodlands always had blue noses. I don't like these sheep with pink noses. They aren't as hardy as blue-nosed Woodlands and they're often too big. We used to be trying to bring down the size of them. Butchers couldn't manage a big side of mutton across the counter. Those with pink noses were often bad on their feet too. Anyway, they used to cross them with Dorsets in those days to try and bring the size of the sheep down.'

74

It should be noted that the Limestone was a much bigger sheep than the Dorset, and, according to Wallace, the Limestone was crossed with the Dorset too for the same reason. We also need to remember that the Limestone died out in popularity in Northern Lancashire and Westmorland because they were pure white, pink-nosed and bad on their feet on wet ground. That is why, according to Garnett, that they were crossed by the Victorians with the black-faced sheep to make them hardier and better on their feet!

'Back in the 1930s the sheep job was down and out. Woodlands died out; they were too big compared with Swaledales and Gritstones. But there was a general lack of interest in sheep altogether.

'In the late 1940s the Woodland breed was nearly wiped out by several bad winters. They had to do something, so it wasn't just the Dorset that was introduced, all sorts of other breeds were also introduced quietly on different farms. One of the main things they were trying to do was bring the size down a bit. Who knows what went on, on the quiet?

'During the War the Ministry of Food took over and they took all that we could produce, but after the War we were still buying store lambs to fatten, buying them in mid-October and fattening them on the moor over winter. We still do today, but they buy stores to fatten over winter but want them away as the grass starts to grow again in the spring. I suppose it helps that winters are milder these days. In the past we'd wait till they'd had time to fill out a bit, and fetch them in to shear, and if they were still too thin, we'd turn them out again.

'We used to put a Suffolk tup onto Woodlands. That was a good fat lamb. Sometimes you need that bit of fresh blood to make a good big lamb.'

'Did you ever try a Texel tup on your Woodlands, Harold?' I asked, but one look of his face was enough to answer that. He shook his head slowly as if I'd said something really daft. 'So you never bothered with any of these modern continental breeds then?'

'No...' he replied with a chuckle; what a daft question from the youth shone out from behind his eyes. That put me in my place!

'I remember some Woodlands used to have a ginger face,' he continued. 'There were ginger-faced Woodlands going back as far as I can remember. Sometimes they had a single black spot too, on the face or leg. Just the one. It was really black, jet black. It was about that big.' (He made a circle with fore finger and thumb about the size of a 50p piece.)

'Only one?' I asked. 'That seems strange, not one or two?'

'No absolutely, only the one, strange really, when you think about it,' he replied firmly.

'Do you ever remember them being grey-faced?' I asked, but judging by his puzzled face I guess that he hadn't. Farey wrote that the Woodlands of Hope were often grey-faced and Wallace and others have commented that the Penistone was often grey-faced too.

'Well, Woodlands would often throw a grey-faced lamb when crossed with other breeds,' Harold replied. 'The pink-nosed, white-faced Woodland is relatively modern; back then they were all blue-nosed or ginger-faced.'

'When you were showing your Woodlands, what achievement are you most proud of?' I asked. Harold paused for a long moment as he thought through this.

'To be honest, I don't have any single prize that stands out in my mind,' he replied. 'We used to horn brand all our lambs. That mark was there forever, unlike these modern ear tags. Anyone can change those you know; cut out the old one and put in a new one, you know. So these days you don't always know who bred the sheep in front of you. But back in my day, you only had to check out the horn brand, because that was with the sheep for life. So when a sheep that you'd bred came into the ring, you knew it was one of yours. When one that I bred won, I always felt very proud. Nowadays it doesn't seem to matter so much who bred the sheep; it's all about who owns it now. Anyone can buy a good sheep, but it takes a good breeder to breed one. So it was always great to see a sheep that you'd bred win in the ring.'

He moved on to talk about the Mass Trespass.

'Then in 1932 they had that "Mass Trespass". They came in to Hayfield station and they all marched up Kinder Hill. The gamekeepers tried to stop them, but it was no use. One keeper ended up in hospital and he died a bit later. Now they are all over the place like lice on a hedgehog.

'They say, "the land belongs to the people" – that's true – but I look after my bit!

'Following the War we used to turn everything out on the moor most of the year, but we'd send some sheep to out winter near to Sheffield. All except the ewe lambs, which we kept back on the moor. We didn't send them because we lost too many.

'We didn't used to worm or fluke sheep in those days like we do now; we're always putting something or other down their throats. Dips have gone expensive too – we used to make dips from creosote and soft soap – can't do that anymore. They've gone expensive and they're too complex anyway. We used to dip just after shearing in June or July before returning everything up to the moor.'

'That was the only time of the year that we had all the sheep in together,' Dorothy added as way of explanation.

'Did you feed them on the moor during the winter?' I asked.

'No, we would wait until the bad weather stopped and then make our way up there and prod at the snow drifts until we found any trapped sheep. In the 1940s we used to have a good dog called Jock. He could find trapped sheep that were still alive; he didn't bother with the dead ones. He'd paw at the snow and carry on until someone dug the sheep out.'

'Did you feed turnips to your sheep?'

'Aye, we fed turnips in the spring, swedes before lambing and mangels after.'

'Did you feed the sheep with silage? Round bales?'

'No, only hay,' Harold replied as if I was barmy. 'We only ever fed hay.'

'Didn't you used to chop turnips up for the sheep?' Dorothy asked.

'No we only ever chopped up hay and straw for the cows, that's all,' Harold replied.

'What sort of cows?' I asked.

'They were just milky types. We used to milk a handful of cows and take the milk around a few local cottages and houses,' Harold explained.

'Mum used to take milk up to the big house when the landlords were here for the shooting,' Dorothy added. 'She had to have it there by 8.00am so they could use it for their breakfasts. She had to carry it up in quart-sized milk cans, and it was over a mile and a half up to the big house.'

The morning passed all too quickly and the managers of the home wanted the residents to come for their lunch, so I had to call it a day; but it was a great day and I enjoyed chatting with Harold and Dorothy very much.

12. THE LADY BOOTH HALL FLOCK

THE OLDEST FLOCK?

In the hills above Hope nestles the quiet valley of Edale. Here in the southern foot hills of Kinder Scout, David Shirt and four generations of his family have been keeping Woodlands since at the very latest 1920! Do you know of any older Woodland flocks? Yes? Then let us know; I'd love to meet them!

The Whitefaced Woodland is an amalgamation of two earlier breeds, the Penistone, from the north east of the High Peak and the Woodlands of Hope. The Shirts' flock is clearly from the hills above Hope, so how fitting would it be for this to be the oldest Woodland flock?

It was a glorious, sunny 5th of November when my wife Heather and I made our way down the Snake Pass, past Lady Bower Reservoir, on our way to visit the Shirt family. The lake was magically clam, reflecting the steep hill sides and a magnificent blue sky above, and so far the autumn of 2014 has been wonderful and warm. The grass at home is still lush and green, which is most unusual for the time of year. And as we drove up the hill above Hope, it was clear that here too, the grass was still growing lush and green despite the lateness of the season.

I was glad to visit David because he wanted to add this great flock to our new Hill Register, and I was happy to inspect them for him, and take the opportunity to visit this beautiful part of the country again. This is not a difficult procedure for either party and the WWSS inspectors are glad to do it at their own expense to support our breed, with only a minimal charge to cover the administration costs. I really hope that we can keep this up and it is a great service to our group!

David and his son, also called David, were extremely well organised, and we followed them to their field where they were keeping the Woodlands back down the hill for tupping, and watched as they quickly erected a catching pen and gathered the flock for inspection, running them through a mobile race so that I could get a good look at each one.

I hope that David doesn't mind me using his as an example, but I'd like you all to know that we have to have tight rules for inspecting sheep, because we as a society need to only register the very best Woodlands if we are to make this whole thing work. So consequently not every sheep passed. This is always difficult, so I took the time to show David what the problem was, and in every case he was good enough to agree with my decision, without question. What a gentleman! But let's be honest, David does not need me, a relative newcomer, to tell him what's what and the vast majority of his sheep passed with no problems at all! We're glad to welcome them into our Hill Register, thank you David and David.

PROFILE - THE LADY BOOTH HALL FLOCK

Flock prefix: Lady Booth Hall
Year started farming: 1920
Size of flock: Medium (21-50)

Name of breeder: David Shirt
Address: Lady Booth Hall Farm, Edale, Hope S33 7ZH
Telephone: 01433 670282

Date of profile: 5th November 2014

Breeding Policy

The tup was turned out on the 5th of November this year, which is usual for the Woodlands, for lambing at the start of April. They are looking for one good lamb per ewe; they sometimes get more, but David would prefer one strong lamb to two dead ones. Because they only have a few (compared to their other flocks), they keep the Woodlands down on the 'green land' rather than the fell.

David keeps the best forty Woodlands pure bred, but any not so good he keeps back and puts to a Suffolk or Charolais tup. The sheep are given feed blocks through winter, but receive no extra feed before lambing apart from hay in late winter when the grass is gone.

Sometimes the ewes go away for winter to the Staffordshire area.

The Woodlands are lambed indoors, after the mules.

The last tup that David used was a James Gill tup, but before that he used Harold Hodgson tups for a lot of years. This year they are using a tup from Clive Mitchell.

Apart from the odd problem with their feet, the Woodlands don't really have any problems.

'Jim Thorn used to tell me years ago that if they have a bit of black on their feet, they're a bit hardier and harder sheep, less prone to foot problems.'

When picking out breeding stock, David looks for, 'Ones that train, with a leg at each corner, plenty of width between their front legs and plenty of length.' Size matters then. 'Square. A bit of depth, top to bottom and a good head.'

'And the wool?'

'I like it a bit tighter really, snod coated, tight coated.'

They like horns to be nice and round and tight to the head, not too wide so that they get the backs of your legs in the race.

David prefers them without a tuft on their head, but, as he says, you do get them don't you. As for eye colour, he's not bothered if they had blue eyes, for example, because he can't see what difference it makes. I only point this out to those who get bogged down in such detail; the importance for David is in a good square sheep, not the small details like tufts on the head or eye colour.

All the sheep are in the Heptavac system, and, apart from worming and an annual liver fluke treatment, they don't really need any other treatments.

On the moor the Woodlands do very well. David's family have kept Woodlands for years and years, and he just wants to keep the breed going.

David Shirt and family with their tup

Farm Details

Year farm started here: 1920
Size of farm: Group D (101-500 ha)
Land classification: LFA
Farm type: Sheep
Other breeds of sheep/livestock: Herdwicks, Swaledales, Mules

Farm Description

Lady Booth Hall Farm is a traditional High Peak hill farm with hill land and in-bye or 'green land' on the flatter lower ground. The higher ground is steep and poor with a lot of coarse grasses and other tough vegetation, but the lower ground is rich and has well-tended grassland with drystone walls higher up and hedges further down the dale towards the lush lands around Hope. Down here trees offer more shelter and the meadows are intermixed with woods and forest and babbling brooks.

13. THE STONY LANE WOODLANDS

THE LEES OF ROCHDALE

Now don't get me wrong, I love Yorkshire and Yorkshire folk - heck I even married a Yorkshire lass - but just sometimes we in Lancashire get a little tired of you lot in the east assuming that you invented everything!

Now take the Whitefaced Woodland for example: I have lost count of the times I have read somewhere that the Whitefaced Woodland comes from the town of Pensitone. Why do we call it the Woodland then, and not the Penistone? They call it the Woodland because the breed comes from the Woodlands of Hope, which is in Derbyshire, is it not? Okay it has Penistone blood in it, but it is still a Woodland, and, as I have been saying for years and years now, it also has Limestone genes in it, and they came originally from Westmorland (which some Yorkshire folk could just about stomach as a footnote to their breed from Penistone, their Yorkshire breed), but that part of Westmorland is now split between Cumbria and Lancashire, and do you know what? That is just unacceptable; it's just too far! How can your own breed of sheep, a sheep which even now, most reading this will still believe to be a Yorkshire breed have anything to do with Lancashire?

So, it gave me the most enormous pleasure and self-satisfaction to visit Edward Lees' farm in the hills above Rochdale (that's Lancashire by the way, folks) to visit another successful sheep breeder who keeps Whitefaced Woodlands in Lancashire!

Now not only does Edward have Woodlands, but his wife Jane's family, the Earnshaws, have been keeping them since before the last World War! How brilliant is that? They might be, if not the oldest flock, certainly they are one of them!

Could it be that Woodlands have been kept in these Lancashire hills for even longer than that?

Edward and I soon get chatting and Edward tells me that he often comes to Bentham Auction Mart (still Yorkshire but just down the road from me), Clitheroe (Lancashire) and Gisburn (Yorkshire) too. Now today that is not that unusual, we can travel quite easily from market to market, but did that also happen before cattle-trailers, before big sheep wagons or trains even? We'll never know for sure, but families tend to have traditions that pass down through generations, and what works for those farming here today probably worked in the past too! So who knows? Perhaps drovers used to bring sheep this way years before we had modern modes of transport.

If sheep were being traded from Bentham, Clitheroe and Gisburn to farms near Rochdale, then there can be no doubt that the now extinct Craven breed would have followed that route. Now the Craven was a Yorkshire breed; just like the Penistone, it had a white face and both ewes and tups were horned, but like the Limestone (to which it was closely related or perhaps even the same breed but just by another name) it had a tuft of white wool between its horns…Sound familiar?

But I digress, you don't want me gloating and saying 'I told you so', you want to read about Edward's flock.

Edward and his family live high up on the hills north of Rochdale. It's a sparse landscape, windswept and bleak. Apart from the rugged terrain and the rugged sheep, the main features in this landscape are the windmills, harnessing the ubiquitous gales that sweep up the valley from the lowlands beyond, and stone built farms clinging to the hillsides.

On top of the world!

The first thing that hits one climbing the road towards the Lees' house (apart from the rocky track belting the underside of the wife's car that is) is how hard it must be to grow anything up here! Lower down the hill the fields were all green and thick with what looked like lush grass and were being grazed by numerous fat lambs, including many very healthy looking Woodlands, but the higher one goes, the poorer the herbage becomes.

Later on, Edward informs me that the Woodlands in the fields that I passed before belong to his father-in-law and brothers-in-law, the Earnshaws.

Edward and his family have a few fields below the fell, and share the hill grazing with the rest of the family.

A few years ago, Edward's tups were being fought over by some of the top breeders in the breed, but he's fallen on harder times since they lost 90 acres of really good fertile lowland pasture down 'somewhere near sea level'; now Edward struggles to get the same results with his stock, confined as they are to such poor soil 800 to 1,000 feet up in the Pennines, where the soil has a pH of four and, whether it is raining or not, the wind blows hard and cold.

The breeding is still there in his sheep; they carry the same genes that they carried before, but now the constant struggle with the coarse vegetation up here has taken its toll on their size and condition, and Edward tells me how difficult it is for him to get any real size into his lambs these days.

But here's the thing, folks, any young sheep coming from up here are going to be hard little things, and put them on some decent grass and they are going to explode into life, blossoming out into the strongest, hardiest of all stock! But I shouldn't be telling you that, because I will certainly be looking to buy some of these gimmers the next time I see them at Bretton!

PROFILE - THE STONY LANE WOODLANDS

Flock prefix: Stony Lane

Year started farming:
Jane's family started in the
1920s

Size of Woodland flock:
Medium (21-50)

Name of breeder: Edward Lee

Address:
Middle Trough Farm
Shawforth
Rochdale
Lancashire
OL12 8XE

Telephone: 01706 853681

Date of profile:
5thNovember 2014

Edward (right) pictured with his son George

Flock History

Edward and Jane started the flock about 25 years ago with 23 hoggs from Jane's father, Billy Earnshaw. As Edward has a busy electrical contracting business to run, it now falls on George, their son, to do much of the day-to-day running of the farm. George is doing an apprenticeship at Myerscough.

Breeding Policy

The tups go out as late as they can, because up here they need to lamb as late as they can, but usually this is around the beginning of November. This year it was later. They lamb mainly outside, and the sheep are only fed a few feed buckets as the grass dies back at the end of winter.

The Lees expect to lamb at about 120%.

Edward selects tups based on what he needs for his own sheep. In recent years he has felt that the horns are starting to get a bit close to their heads; so next time he will be buying a tup with wider horns to try and counter this.

Edward wants his sheep to have a tight fleece to keep out the weather. He'd like big sheep, but up here that is a difficult thing to do working with this acid soil, and he has found that really fat sheep or heavy-boned sheep have come to the farm and not stood up to the harsh conditions here as well as they could. He finds that his thinner-boned, smaller sheep do better in the long run than ones that arrive in much heavier condition. It is always difficult bringing sheep up the hill. But going the other way, these sheep will be hard!

Tight fleeces and tight horns with a sheep at the back showing a tuft between the horns, is that the Craven in it coming through?

Farm Details

Year farm started: 1992
Size of farm: Group D (101-500 ha)
Land classification: LFA
Altitude: 800 – 1,000ft above sea level

Farm Description

The farm has about 50 acres of lower land, but most of the sheep are kept on the moor above for most of the year with the Earnshaw family's sheep. Here the grass is coarse and full of bent grass and rushes. Even the lower fields, while they looked green enough on the day we visited, are poor quality, tough grasses.

With a pH of somewhere around four it is very acid and peaty. It is also wet and boggy and full of soft rushes.

The sheep's fleeces show lots of colour from the peaty soil.

14. THE BARNSFOLD FLOCK

THROUGH THE MIST

Doing these flock profiles is sometimes like driving down a misty road in autumn; one rarely goes into a profile completely blind, one usually knows the person being visited, briefly. One's seen them at shows or sales, or one knows them by reputation, but one has never seen the whole picture. So it was with Tony Redfern and his father-in-law and business partner, Simon Burford: I have met them both and seen Tony winning the Ken Wild Memorial trophy at Bretton Mill, but that doesn't mean that I knew what to expect exactly. Of course, I knew they had some good sheep - that was a given - but were they just selecting a good sheep from hundreds? Or did they have just a small handful of excellent Woodlands amidst hundreds of Swaledales? I just didn't know quite what to expect.

It is also rare to go to a farm and get to see the whole flock all in one go. It's just like driving through patchy mist again as the flock is revealed to me. Usually I'm shown just a few sheep at a time, rarely the whole flock at once; so the visit is a journey too, just like driving through patchy mist as the truth about the flock is revealed.

Well it wasn't quite that way with Tony, but the first thing he did say to me was that these weren't his best sheep. He then told me what a mess the building was in that we were going to use to look at them, and when I asked if I could take a few pictures of the pens, he laughed and said, 'No, not this rubbish' (or words to that effect). But here's the thing, these old dusty pens were beautifully made. They were not just a load of old broken pallets like the ones we use; these were made by a craftsman. Someone had taken a lot of time and trouble to make proper joints and bevel all the edges. What Tony dismissed as rubbish was anything but!

Tony being awarded the Ken Wild Trophy in 2011 at Bretton by Neville Belfield

This early discussion set the tone of the whole visit, because it soon became clear to me that Tony is a perfectionist. As his sheep came in and we started to inspect them I soon came to realise that the reason Tony is at the top of his game is because of attention to detail. Quite frankly, I would be happy to own any of his sheep.

Talking with Tony as we went through the first flock, I grew to realise that Tony was not just looking for big impressive sheep (show stoppers if you like), Tony wanted his flock to be good commercial sheep.

Tony being presented with the Ken Wild Memorial Trophy by Beth Wild, judged by James Gill, in 2014

Well we all want that, don't we? Well no, not really, some of the farms that I have visited before have a commercial flock and a show flock. The commercial sheep do one thing, and the show flock another. Not Tony's flock, Tony is building a whole flock of good commercial sheep. He does not really show his sheep except at Hayfield (to support his local show) and when selling tups at Bretton Mill, yet here he stands his ground against some of the best Woodlands anywhere and wins. What does that tell you? Well, it tells me that this is one of the most consistent flocks that I have ever seen anywhere … and then we moved on to the next flock, his 'better' sheep and guess what, folks, yes they were better as a whole, but once again they were consistent with the first flock, and all the time it was clear that this was down to attention to detail. It was like coming out of the mist and seeing a bright clear view in front of me. I finally understood why Tony wins at Bretton Mill. Tony Redfern is what we up here call 'real'; he is a real stockman.

PROFILE -THE BARNSFOLD FLOCK

Flock prefix: Barnsfold

Size of Woodland flock:
Major (101+)

Name of breeders:
Tony Redfern and
Simon Burford

Address:
Booth Farm
Kinder Rd
Hayfield

Telephone: 07813054283

Date of profile:
13th November 2014

Breeding Policy

Tony is looking for good sheep first and foremost, solid but not necessarily heavily-boned. Actually, Tony is not a fan of heavy-boned Woodlands; he thinks that they tend to be too heavy and that makes them down on their pasterns and dip in the backs. He wants his sheep to have tight fleeces and look 'clean', by which I understood him to mean even-coated, without tufts and lumps of wool sticking out here and there.

All morning I only saw one sheep with any colour on its face and that only had the slightest freckling, so clearly pink noses count for something.

Tony is looking for broad sheep and longer sheep, but he doesn't want them too deep in the body. The result of this was a very even size to all the ewes, not too big and not small. It's meaty sheep he wants, not bone, belly or wool.

In selecting tups, Tony is very particular; he does not want them too heavy, down on their pasterns or dipping heavily in the back. Again, he is looking at sheep that will produce meat, not wool, bone or fat

As for horns, these are last on Tony's list for importance.

Farm Details

Size of farm: Group D (101-500 ha)
Land classification: LFA
Other breeds of sheep/livestock: Swaledales, Gritstones and Woodland Halfbreds

Farm Description

The farm is divided between two main sites. Each site is high up on the hillsides above Hayfield and towards Kinder Scout. The in-bye land is green and lush compared to the steep hillsides above. The soil is acidic and poor and in places, wet and soft. While some fields are well drained and firm, others are very wet.

The Woodlands are kept mainly on the higher ground where, Tony says, they tend to go to. When gathering them, apparently the Woodlands are right on the top, while Swaledales come down the slopes to the lower ground.

Flock Management

The management of the Woodlands is in line with them being a commercial flock; they are only fed extra as really needed to keep costs down to an absolute minimum.

They are bred and managed to maximise outputs from the poorest of land, relying on conformation and good breeding to do the work for them.

CONCLUDING NOTE

Writing these flock profiles has been a rare privilege, and I am extremely grateful to all the breeders featured in this book for allowing me to visit them and profile their flocks. Collectively they have given me a unique view of some of the hidden facets of the Whitefaced Woodland world, and, hopefully, for those who read them I have been able to pass some of that knowledge on.

I should point out a number of things that qualify these profiles, however:

- Not every important flock owner has allowed me access to their flocks, and some that did declined the offer for me to profile their flock.

- I have visited and examined more flocks than those that are profiled here.

- I have published what the breeders told me and none of this has been verified scientifically.

- I have published the breeders' viewpoints, which does not necessarily mean that I agree with or endorse them here. While all talked of 'good' horns, heads, wool, backs and so on, what each person actually meant by these terms was not always the same thing!

Finally, readers who are interested in technical details of the inspection process for Whitefaced Woodlands (which was developed for the Whitefaced Woodland Sheep Society after extensive discussions with them and members from the Rare Breeds Survival Trust) can download, without charge, a pdf copy of the inspection guide I have written from my website at: http://www.keerfalls.co.uk/GoodWW.html